Working Mom's
FAST & EASY
ONE-POT
COOKING

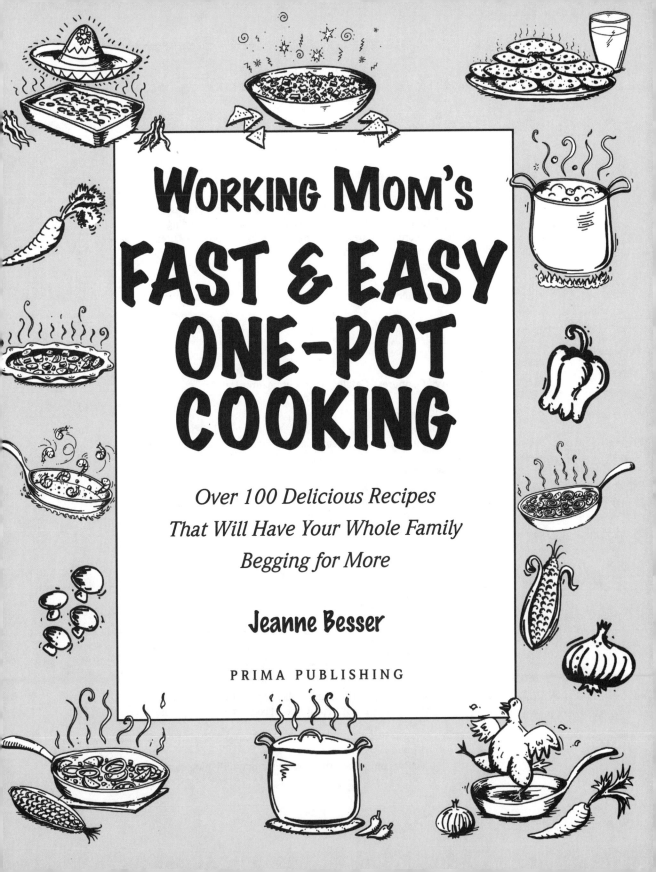

WORKING MOM'S
FAST & EASY
ONE-POT
COOKING

Over 100 Delicious Recipes
That Will Have Your Whole Family
Begging for More

Jeanne Besser

PRIMA PUBLISHING

Products mentioned in this book are trademarks of their respective companies.

PRIMA PUBLISHING and colophon are registered trademarks of Prima Communications, Inc.

Library of Congress Cataloging-in-Publication Data

Besser, Jeanne
    Working mom's fast & easy one-pot cooking : over 100 delicious recipes that will have your whole family begging for more / Jeanne Besser
        p.   cm.
    Includes index.
    ISBN 0-7615-1432-5
    1. Entrées (Cookery). 2. Casserole cookery. 3. Soups. 4. Stews.
5. Quick and easy cookery. I. Title.
TX740.B4918   1998
641.8′2—dc21   98-26037
                                                                        CIP

    99 00 01 HH 10 9 8 7 6 5 4 3

Printed in the United States of America

How to Order
Single copies may be ordered from Prima Publishing, P.O. Box 1260BK, Rocklin, CA 95677; telephone (916) 632-4400. Quantity discounts are also available. On your letterhead, include information concerning the in-tended use of the books and the number of books you wish to purchase.

Visit us online at http://www.primapublishing.com

To Rich, Alex, and Jack
for new beginnings

To Sarah
for her courage and inspiration

Contents

Chapter 3 • Meat   41

Chapter 4 • Seafood   69

60 Minutes or Less:

Chapter 5 · Vegetarian   101

30 Minutes or Less:

60 Minutes or Less:

Chapter 6 • Weekend Cooking   139

Poultry

Meat

Chapter 7 · Salads   165

Chapter 8 · Desserts   181

Acknowledgments

I'd like to thank Jamie Miller for bringing this book to life, and Andi Reese Brady and Naomi Lucks for their editorial contributions. Thanks to Linda Martin, Jodi Long, Rosemary Rossi, Sarah François Poncet, and Lorraine Phillips, for their friendship. To great testers and friends: Jolene Kriett, Pamela Racliff, Bill Perry, DeeAnne and Michael Canepa, Lauren and Derrick Cartwright, David Weinman, and Linda Coulter. To George and Jean Jackson for their generosity; Nancy McCarten for her mouth-watering e-mails; and Bert Hoberman, Ruth Besser, and Howard Taras for their recipes.

And most of all, thank you to my families, the Hobermans and the Bessers.

Introduction

If you are like me—a working mom with a family to feed and not much time to do it in—you need a way to prepare dinner without spending the whole day in the kitchen and the whole night cleaning up. Let me share my secret for simplifying mealtime without sacrificing quality: one-pot cooking. Not the kind of one-pot recipes that eventually end up in one pot after cooking everything separately; I mean one pot, period. Just one pot to cook in and just one pot to wash.

From the hearty and comforting stews of yesteryear to the quicker and lighter fare favored today, you will find a wide assortment of easy-to-prepare, low-maintenance, nutritious one-pot stews, soups, chilis, gumbos, curries, casseroles, pastas, risottos, quiches, and more. These meals are very forgiving, with few repercussions for taking a break to referee a battle between siblings or answer an unexpected phone call from a child's teacher.

In addition to over 100 recipes, *Working Mom's Fast & Easy One-Pot Cooking* also includes helpful hints for quickly getting your food on the table, advice on how to choose equipment and ingredients, and ways to better organize your kitchen.

Whether you're looking for a casual dinner or an elegant meal for entertaining, *Working Mom's Fast & Easy One-Pot Cooking* lets you take back your life without forfeiting flavor.

Chart of Equivalents

Use this handy reference to help you know how much food to shop for.

1 cup = 8 ounces
1 pound = 16 ounces

1 cup cored and coarsely chopped apple = 4 ounces
1 cup cored and sliced apple = 5 ounces
1 cup sliced asparagus (1-inch pieces) = 5 ounces
1 cup packed basil leaves = 2 ounces
1 cup 1-inch-cubed butternut squash = 5 ounces
1 cup sliced carrots = 5 ounces
1 cup finely chopped carrots = 4 ounces
1 cup coarsely chopped celery = 4 ounces
1 cup shredded cheese = 4 ounces
1 cup coarsely chopped cucumber = 5 ounces
1 cup coarsely chopped eggplant = 2½ ounces
1 cup sliced green beans (1-inch pieces) = 4 ounces
1 cup chopped bell peppers = 4 ounces
1 cup sliced leeks, white part only = 2 ounces
1 cup packed lettuce = 2 ounces
1 cup chopped mushrooms = 3 ounces
1 cup quartered mushrooms = 4 ounces
1 cup sliced mushrooms = 2½ ounces
1 cup coarsely chopped onions = 5 ounces
1 cup ½-inch-cubed potatoes = 6 ounces

1 cup thinly sliced potatoes = 5 ounces
1 cup shredded potatoes = 3½ ounces
1 cup sliced shiitake mushrooms = 2 ounces
1 cup snow pea pods = 3 ounces
1 cup packed spinach = 1½ ounces
1 cup chopped and seeded fresh tomatoes = 5½ ounces
1 cup ½-inch-cubed turnips = 4 ounces
1 cup ½-inch-cubed zucchini = 4 ounces

Chart of Equivalents

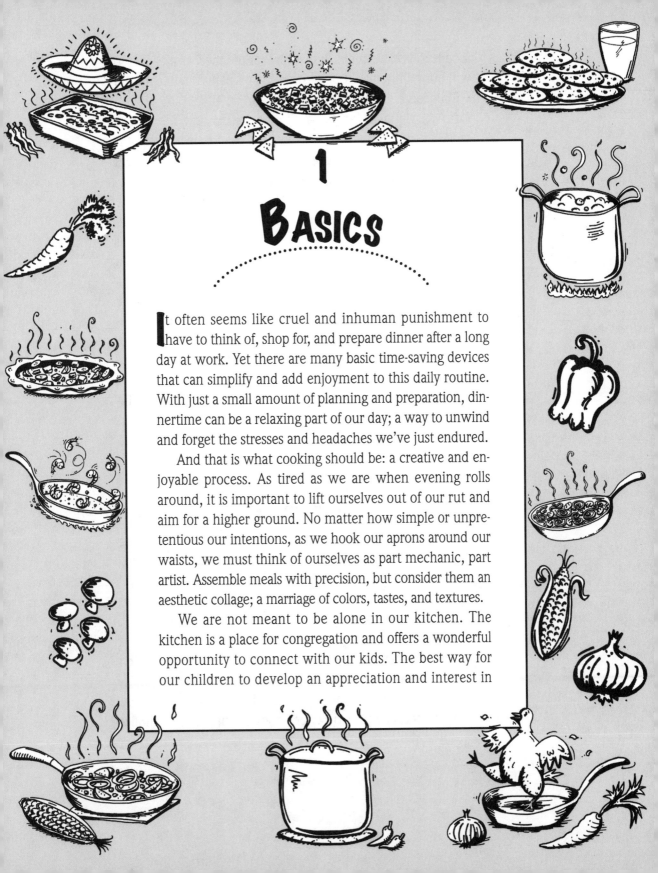

1

BASICS

It often seems like cruel and inhuman punishment to have to think of, shop for, and prepare dinner after a long day at work. Yet there are many basic time-saving devices that can simplify and add enjoyment to this daily routine. With just a small amount of planning and preparation, dinnertime can be a relaxing part of our day; a way to unwind and forget the stresses and headaches we've just endured.

And that is what cooking should be: a creative and enjoyable process. As tired as we are when evening rolls around, it is important to lift ourselves out of our rut and aim for a higher ground. No matter how simple or unpretentious our intentions, as we hook our aprons around our waists, we must think of ourselves as part mechanic, part artist. Assemble meals with precision, but consider them an aesthetic collage; a marriage of colors, tastes, and textures.

We are not meant to be alone in our kitchen. The kitchen is a place for congregation and offers a wonderful opportunity to connect with our kids. The best way for our children to develop an appreciation and interest in food is to involve them. If we think of the meal as a chore, so will our children. But if we make its preparation an event, it will become exciting for all. Let them smell the spices, perform simple tasks, and choose creative decorations for the table. Even toddlers relish the tasks of food preparation. Stirring and pushing the buttons of a food processor allows them to be a part of the creative process.

Variety takes the monotony out of cooking. The more we expose children to a diversity of food, the more interested and adventurous eaters they will become. Expand their minds and their tastebuds. It is exciting to be able to travel using just our imaginations and our palate. Explore recipes from different regions of the country and from around the world and turn dinnertime into a geography lesson. While we're cooking up specialties from Mexico, Greece, Morocco, Italy, and France, we can discuss their cultures and locate them on the globe.

Let's begin our culinary journey with a guide to basic information and time-tested tips to help ensure success. As you read through the following pointers and techniques, try to take from them things that will work in your own kitchen.

Equipment:

- Buy the best quality equipment you can afford. Sturdier equipment will last longer, and higher quality, heavy cookware will prevent unnecessary scorching and overcooking.
- For simplicity, I have limited the number of pots and pans necessary. For a soup pot and pasta pot, I used an 8-quart stock pot; for a large sauté pan, I used a 13-inch skillet; for a smaller frying pan, I used a 10-inch nonstick skillet. Dutch ovens (heavy porcelain- or enamel-coated cooking vessels) are excellent for stove-to-oven use. They can be substituted for the pots and pans described above if they are of a similar

size or capacity. For oven use I recommend a 9-inch pie pan and a $13 \times 9 \times 2$-inch baking pan (this is a little big for four servings, but 8- or 9-inch square pans are too small). While nonstick cookware makes cleanup easier and cuts down on the amount of fat needed, they are not essential unless specifically noted.

- Before choosing your cookware, review the recipe and note if a cover is needed or if the pot needs to be ovenproof. Ovenproof pots must have handles that can withstand high heat. Whenever removing a pan from the oven, remember to use extreme caution: The pan will continue to hold its heat for a long time. I like to leave a pot holder or mitt on top of pots and lids removed from the oven as a reminder not to touch.

- A food processor is helpful for chopping and slicing large amounts of vegetables and for puréeing soups. It is important when chopping vegetables with a high water content, like onions or bell peppers, to only pulse small amounts at a time or the vegetables will end up a pulverized mush.

- Invest in an oven thermometer to make sure your oven is heating properly. A hanging mercury thermometer is most reliable. Check the temperature in different areas of your oven to make sure it has consistent heat. If you notice heating discrepancies, adjust your cooking time or temperature to compensate. Most utility companies will recalibrate your oven at no cost.

Ingredients:

- Always use high quality ingredients. If something doesn't taste good by itself, it won't taste better after cooking. Make sure vegetables and fruits are ripe and flavorful; dairy products, meats, poultry, and fish are fresh; and flavorings are the best available. Use fresh and fragrant herbs and spices. Store dried spices tightly covered in a cool and dry place for better and longer-lasting flavor. If spices are no longer aromatic, replace them.

- Most of these recipes call for fresh vegetables and herbs. Frozen vegetables may be substituted if necessary, but the texture and flavor may suffer. One exception to the "fresh-is-best" rule is the recommended use of canned tomatoes, because flavorful tomatoes are only in season for a short amount of time. Fresh tomatoes can be substituted for canned tomatoes when they are ripe and in season. The general rule of thumb for substituting dried herbs for fresh is to use one-third of the recommended amount. Many of these recipes use fresh herbs for their unique flavor, and a dried-for-fresh substitution would be lacking. So if fresh herbs are not available, just leave them out.

- Be flexible and cook for your own tastes. Cooking allows for a lot of adaptation. If you like your food extra hot, increase the cayenne pepper by a shake or two. If you don't like one of the ingredients in a recipe, or if a particular vegetable is unavailable, substitute one of your favorites that complements the dish. Just alter the cooking time, if necessary, to make up for added or decreased weight.

- Never cook with a wine you wouldn't enjoy drinking on its own. As wine cooks, its flavor intensifies. The wine doesn't need to be expensive, but it must be drinkable. If you wish to cook without alcohol, substitute an equal amount of compatible broth.

- Some recipes list optional ingredients or garnishes. While they will heighten the flavor and presentation of the dish, these ingredients are not essential. The finished meal won't suffer if you are missing them, but it will be enhanced by their inclusion. Recipe introductions sometimes offer complementary toppings and side suggestions. Again, you can choose whether or not to use them.

- Some manufacturers' canned items may vary from ¼ to ½ ounce from what is used in the recipe. This will not affect the outcome of the meal. Just use whatever you can find that is closest to the recommended size.
- Personalize your cookbooks to use as a guide for your future cooking. On the recipe, note if there are any additions or changes you would make for next time.

Before Starting the Recipe:

- Always read through the entire recipe to make sure all the ingredients are on hand and to see if additional preparation is needed (chopping, peeling, toasting, and so on). Measuring and prepping your ingredients before beginning to cook will eliminate any surprises halfway into the recipe and will save a lot of time and aggravation later on. Additionally, a more organized preparation makes for an easier cleanup.
- Another helpful technique is to line up the ingredients on your work space, in the order in which they are listed in the recipe, before starting the recipe. Move the ingredient aside after it has been used. This ensures nothing has been forgotten or added twice. To prevent accidental overflows, never measure ingredients over mixing bowls or over the cooking pan.
- Most ingredients in this book are measured by standard measurers (cups, teaspoons, tablespoons). I feel this means is the most practical for home cooks for two reasons. First, measuring cups and spoons are universal, but everyone's perception of a "large" tomato is different. What is large to one may seem medium to another. Second, many ingredients are now sold prepped to eliminate additional work, whether it be jarred minced garlic, packaged cut-up lettuce, or salad bar shredded vegetables. Although weighing ingredients is the most accurate method of measuring, most

homes are not equipped with the scales necessary to make this a practical means of calculation. But when an item is used whole or needs minimal prep, or if it is sold by weight, like cheese or meat, than a size or weight description is provided. An equivalency guide is included on page xvii to aid in shopping.

- Use these approximate guidelines for cutting descriptions:
  minced: $\frac{1}{16}$ inch or under
  chopped: $\frac{1}{8}$ inch to $\frac{1}{4}$ inch
  coarsely chopped: $\frac{1}{4}$ inch to $\frac{1}{2}$ inch
  thinly sliced: $\frac{1}{8}$ inch or under
  sliced: $\frac{1}{8}$ inch to $\frac{1}{4}$ inch
  thickly sliced: $\frac{1}{4}$ inch
  julienned : cut into 1- to 2-inch pieces and sliced thinly
    lengthwise
  cubed: cut into $\frac{1}{2} \times \frac{1}{2}$-inch or 1×1-inch squares

Planning Ahead:

- You can save valuable time by using a little foresight. Before shopping, look through your cupboards, refrigerator, and freezer, and plan your meals to use up what you have on hand.
- Keep your kitchen well stocked with staples for cooking in a pinch. Remember to replenish what you use by adding it to your shopping list immediately.
- Organize your kitchen to shorten your prep time. Divide your cupboard into sections and keep frequently used canned goods, condiments, cooking oils, and spices visible and arranged by categories. The easier it is to find things, the quicker it will be to make your meal.
- Prepare your vegetables at the beginning of the week. Chop several onions, slice carrots and celery, and mince a head of garlic. Then store each separately, in airtight containers,

Basics

until needed. Any leftover veggies are great in salads or simple stir-fries. If time is short, shop for pre-cut vegetables at your supermarket's salad bar.

- If you are preparing rice or pasta for a dinner, cook an extra batch to enhance a future one-pot meal. Save and freeze leftover rice from Chinese take-out meals. If you feel like adding rice to a dish, it's just a quick microwave away!

- If you find a recipe you enjoy, make a double batch and freeze half for a later date. Doubling a recipe does not double the work.

Keeping Clean:

- The more organized your kitchen is while you are preparing the recipe, the easier it will be to keep clean. After cooking, return things to their proper place so they will be accessible the next time you need them.

- Keep a trash receptacle close by and deposit all used wrappers and waste immediately. If a trash can isn't handy, place an empty box, grocery bag, or mixing bowl near your work space.

- Always use larger mixing bowls than you think will be necessary to eliminate messy spills and overflows. This also prevents the need to transfer ingredients to a larger bowl midway through the recipe, requiring additional cleanup.

Freezing:

- Most soups, stews, and casseroles freeze beautifully when wrapped airtight using foil, plastic wrap, zip-top bags, or plastic containers. Make sure the wrap and bags are intended for freezer use.

- Label and date everything before freezing so you can use it in a timely fashion. Keep a current list of freezer contents to refresh your memory.

Salads and Breads:

- A side salad and bread are the perfect complements to most one-pot dishes.
- Try making your own bread, or experiment with supermarket or bakery varieties until you find your favorites.
- Look for crusty French and Italian breads or a hearty multi-grain loaf to round out your meal and help guests capture every last drop of your sensational soups, stews, and sauces.
- Serve breads from other countries—including pita, focaccia, garlic bread, bruschetta, and tortillas—to tie into international-theme dinners.
- For fun, serve a variety of different shaped breads, including rolls, fogossi (a shaped bread), and bread sticks.

2

POULTRY

30 Minutes or Less:

Mulligatawny Soup
Southwest Chicken
    Tortilla Soup
Moroccan Chicken with
    Couscous

Chicken Pesto Risotto
Chicken Caesar Salad
    Wrap
Thai Chicken Salad Wrap

60 Minutes or Less:

Chicken and Vegetables
Chicken Chili
Mediterranean Chicken
    and Rice
Brunswick Stew
Spicy Pepper Chicken
Curried Chicken and Rice

Chicken Cacciatore
Chicken and Barley Stew
Arroz con Pollo
Creamy Dijon Chicken
    Stew
Turkey, Potatoes,
    Tomatoes, and Cheese

Poultry, long favored by cooks for its versatility, is also a nutritional winner. Low in fat and calories, as well as a good source of B_2, B_6, B_{12}, riboflavin, niacin, zinc, and magnesium, poultry is also widely available and relatively inexpensive. Whether you choose a whole chicken or Rock Cornish hens for roasting; a cut-up fryer for braising or stewing; or boneless breasts or thighs for easy sautés and soup-making, poultry is a great centerpiece for family one-pot dinners.

Poultry Tips:

- Always check the expiration date before buying packaged poultry. Look for plump, meaty pieces so you pay for bulk, not just bone or skin.
- Be aware of the possible bacterial contamination of poultry. Salmonella and campylobacter are the two pathogens most commonly associated with raw chicken. Before using chicken, carefully rinse it with cold water (making sure it doesn't spray all over the counters) and cut off any excess fat and skin. After cutting or handling raw chicken, always thoroughly wash your hands, counters, cutting boards, and knives with warm, soapy water. Store uncooked chicken separately from other ingredients to prevent cross-contamination. These bacteria are killed with proper cooking.
- Store poultry in your refrigerator. If you are unable to use poultry within three days or by its expiration date, it is best to freeze it. To prevent bacterial growth, always thaw chicken in your refrigerator or microwave, not at room temperature.
- If you find you have more chicken than you need for your meal, wrap, label, and store the extra in the freezer.
- For better browning, always pat the chicken dry with paper towels before searing. Sear chicken pieces a few at a

time—if you overcrowd the pan, the chicken will steam rather than brown.

- When cooking a cut-up fryer, remember that dark meat (the thighs and legs) generally takes about ten to fifteen minutes longer to cook than white meat. Check the pieces as they are cooking. If some are done before others, remove them and tent with aluminum foil to keep warm. Chicken is done when a meat thermometer inserted into the inner thigh registers 170 to 180 degrees and juices run clear, not pink.

- Even when cooking with all white meat or all dark meat, adjust the cooking time if you have pieces of greatly varying sizes. Larger pieces of meat will take longer to cook than smaller ones (sometimes an exceptionally big breast will take more time than a large piece of dark meat). Check pieces for doneness as they are cooking, or add smaller pieces ten minutes after larger pieces have been cooking. If you are using boneless and skinless chicken breasts of irregular thickness, either pound them for uniform density or alter their cooking times accordingly to prevent dried-out meat.

- Substitute individual chicken parts for a whole chicken if your family's preference is all white or all dark meat.

- To prevent tough and chewy chicken, cook at a simmer, not a boil.

- Before serving stews, use a soup spoon or paper towels to skim off any fat or froth that has risen to the surface, or run an ice cube over the surface to quickly solidify any liquid fat. If you are cooking and refrigerating the stew, the fat will harden when chilled and is easily removed.

- Add leftover chicken to vegetarian entreés for extra protein.

Mulligatawny Soup

2 tablespoons butter
1 cup chopped onions
1 cup chopped carrots
½ cup chopped celery
1 cup peeled, cored, and
      chopped Granny Smith
      apples
2 tablespoons all-purpose flour
1 tablespoon curry powder
⅛ teaspoon ground cloves
5 cups reduced-sodium
      chicken broth
1 cup peeled, seeded, and
      chopped ripe
      tomatoes, or 1 cup
      drained canned diced
      tomatoes
1 tablespoon freshly squeezed
      lemon juice
½ cup rice
1 pound boneless and skinless
      chicken breasts, cut
      into ½-inch pieces
1 teaspoon salt
½ teaspoon ground black
      pepper

This curried chicken soup, a classic eighteenth-century East Indian favorite, is flavored with apples, lemon, and cloves. Literally translated as "pepper water," Mulligatawny was originally made by Indian cooks for British colonialists, who later brought the recipe back to England and then to the United States. It is normally served with a side of rice, but this recipe cooks the rice right into the soup. Optional garnishes include a dollop of yogurt, grated apple, or a sprinkling of parsley.

Cooking Time: 30 minutes or less
Serves: 4

1. In a large stock pot over medium heat, add the butter. Add the onions, carrots, celery, and apples and cook until softened, 5 to 8 minutes, stirring occasionally.
2. Add the flour, curry, and cloves and cook for 1 to 2 minutes, stirring constantly.
3. Add the broth, tomatoes, and lemon juice and stir to combine. Bring to a boil.
4. Add the rice and stir to combine.

Poultry

5. Reduce the heat, partially cover, and simmer for 10 minutes, stirring occasionally.
6. Add the chicken. Simmer for 5 to 10 minutes, or until the chicken and rice are cooked through. Season with salt and pepper.

Southwest Chicken Tortilla Soup

1 tablespoon vegetable oil
½ cup chopped onions
1 teaspoon minced garlic
½ teaspoon chili powder
⅛ teaspoon cayenne pepper
4 cups reduced-sodium
    chicken broth
1 cup canned Mexican-style
    stewed tomatoes
1 teaspoon salt
1 pound boneless and skinless
    chicken breasts, cut
    into ½-inch pieces
1 cup fresh or frozen corn
¼ cup thinly sliced scallions
2 tablespoons freshly
    squeezed lime juice
4 6-inch corn tortillas, lightly
    toasted and sliced into
    ½-inch strips, or 2
    cups crushed tortilla
    chips

This Mexican-inspired soup has found a loyal following north of the border. Full of tender chicken, corn, and tomatoes, it has a little spice and a lot of flavor. Garnish with sour cream or chopped cilantro, and serve with warm flour tortillas topped with melted Monterey Jack cheese and a tossed salad loaded with avocado.

Cooking Time: 30 minutes or less
Serves: 4

1. In a large stock pot over medium heat, add the oil. Add the onions and cook until softened, 3 to 5 minutes, stirring frequently.
2. Add the garlic, chili powder, and cayenne pepper and cook for 1 minute, stirring constantly.
3. Add the broth, tomatoes and their juice, and salt, and stir to combine and to break up the tomatoes. Bring to a boil.
4. Reduce the heat, cover, and simmer for 10 to 15 minutes, stirring occasionally.
5. Add the chicken and corn and simmer for 5 minutes.

6. Add the scallions and lime juice and cook for 1 minute, or until the chicken is cooked through.
7. Top each serving with the tortillas.

•••••••••••••••••

Variation:

Southwest Shrimp Tortilla Soup: *Substitute ¾ pound of peeled and deveined shrimp for the chicken. Add the shrimp in step 6 and cook for 1 to 2 minutes, or until just cooked through.*

•••••••••••••••••

Moroccan Chicken with Couscous

1 teaspoon salt
¼ teaspoon cayenne pepper
1 teaspoon ground ginger
1 teaspoon ground cumin
1 teaspoon ground cinnamon
½ teaspoon ground coriander
    (optional)
4 boneless and skinless
    chicken breasts (about
    1½ pounds)
2 tablespoons olive oil
1 cup finely chopped onions
½ cup finely chopped carrots
½ cup seeded and finely
    chopped red bell
    peppers
1 teaspoon minced garlic
2 cups reduced-sodium
    chicken broth
2 tablespoons freshly
    squeezed lemon juice
1½ cups couscous
½ cup rinsed and drained
    canned chickpeas
¼ cup pitted and halved green
    olives
½ cup pine nuts, lightly
    toasted (optional)

This fast and low-fat meal features chicken breasts coated with the spices of Morocco. At first glance these flavorings seem unusual partners: cinnamon and ginger, normally associated with baking; and cayenne, cumin, and coriander, normally found in savory Indian cooking. But when wed, they burst with exciting flavors. Couscous, this version jazzed up with onions, carrots, and red bell peppers, is a mainstay of this region.

Cooking Time: 30 minutes or less
Serves: 4

1. Combine the salt, cayenne pepper, ginger, cumin, cinnamon, and coriander. Coat the chicken with the spices.
2. In a large skillet over medium-high heat, add the oil. Add the chicken and brown, 4 to 5 minutes per side. Remove the chicken, cover with foil, and reserve.
3. Add the onions, carrots, red peppers, and garlic and cook until softened, 5 to 8 minutes, stirring frequently.
4. Add the broth and lemon juice and stir to combine. Bring to a boil.

5. Turn off the heat, add the couscous, chickpeas, and olives and stir to combine. Return the chicken to the skillet, cover, and let stand for 5 to 10 minutes.
6. Fluff the couscous and top with the pine nuts.

Chicken Pesto Risotto

4 to 5 cups reduced-sodium
 chicken broth
3 tablespoons butter
½ cup finely chopped onions
1 teaspoon minced garlic
½ pound boneless and skinless
 chicken breasts, cut
 into 1-inch pieces
1½ cups Arborio rice
½ cup dry white wine
½ cup pesto, ready-made or
 recipe, page 14
¼ cup shaved or grated
 Parmesan cheese

Risotto demands vigilance: The slow absorption of broth is integral to the creamy, yet firm, quality of the finished dish. But a beautiful restaurant-quality risotto, made with Italian Arborio rice, can be on your dinner table in half an hour or less, so it's definitely worth the effort. This Chicken Pesto Risotto is bursting with flavor. Make the pesto in the height of summer when basil is abundant, or use ready-made pesto in a pinch. One note: It is not essential to warm the broth first, but it does help maintain a constant cooking temperature.

Cooking Time: 30 minutes or less
Serves: 4

1. In a microwave, bring the broth to a simmer.
2. In a large saucepan or stock pot over medium heat, add the butter. Add the onions, garlic, and chicken and sauté for 3 to 5 minutes, or until the chicken begins to cook through, stirring frequently.
3. Add the rice. Stir constantly to coat with the butter, 1 minute.
4. Add the wine and stir until completely absorbed.
5. Begin slowly adding the broth, ½ cup at a time, stirring frequently. Wait until each addition is almost

completely absorbed before adding more, about 3 to 5 minutes for each addition. Continue to add broth, stirring frequently, for 20 to 25 minutes, or until the risotto has a creamy texture but is still al dente, slightly firm to the bite. You may not need to use all of the liquid.

6. Transfer the risotto to a serving dish. Stir in the pesto. Sprinkle with the Parmesan and serve immediately.

. . . .

Variation:

Shrimp Pesto Risotto: *Substitute ¾ pound of peeled and deveined shrimp for the chicken. Proceed with the recipe through step 5. Add the shrimp after 15 minutes. Continue adding broth and stirring for another 5 to 8 minutes.*

. . . .

Chicken Caesar Salad Wrap

Dressing:

1 clove garlic
½ cup olive oil
¼ cup mayonnaise
2 tablespoons freshly
    squeezed lemon juice
2 teaspoons Dijon mustard
1 teaspoon Worcestershire
    sauce
1 teaspoon anchovy paste,
    chopped anchovies,
    or salt
1 teaspoon ground black
    pepper

4 boneless and skinless
    chicken breasts (about
    1½ pounds)
1 tablespoon olive oil
4 10- to 12-inch flour tortillas

Salad:

5 cups packed chopped
    romaine lettuce
½ cup shaved or grated
    Parmesan cheese
1 cup croutons
1 cup chopped ripe tomatoes
    (optional)

Wraps, healthful and flavorful cross-cultural sandwiches, are currently the hottest category in casual dining. Tastes from all over the world mix and mingle in these trendy sandwiches. The Caesar wrap is a perfect example. The original Caesar salad was created by Italian chef Caesar Cardini in 1924 at his restaurant in Tijuana, Mexico. Many Americans frequented the border towns at this time because of Prohibition, and word of this tasty salad quickly traveled north with them. Its trademark dressing, loaded with garlic, lemon, and Parmesan cheese, is easy to make; but if time is short, substitute your favorite bottled dressing.

Cooking Time: 30 minutes or less
Serves: 4

1. Preheat the broiler or grill.
2. Prepare the dressing: In a food processor fitted with a metal chopping blade, with the motor running, add the garlic and purée. Add the oil, mayonnaise, lemon juice, mustard, Worcestershire sauce, anchovy paste, and pepper and process to combine. (You can also mix the dressing in a bowl using a wire whisk). Set aside.
3. Lightly brush the chicken with the oil. Broil or grill the chicken breasts, 4 to 5 minutes per side, or until cooked through. When cool, cut the chicken into thin strips and set aside.

Poultry

4. If using a broiler, lower the heat to 350 degrees; if using a grill reduce heat to low. Wrap the tortillas in aluminum foil and place in the oven or on the grill to warm for 10 minutes. (Tortillas can also be wrapped in a damp towel and warmed in the microwave on high for 15 to 30 seconds).

5. Prepare the salad: In a large bowl, combine the lettuce and dressing. Add the cheese, croutons, tomatoes, and chicken and toss again.

6. Assemble the wraps: Place 1 to 1½ cups of salad in the center of each tortilla. Tuck the bottom of the tortilla up over the filling, fold both sides of the tortilla toward the center, and roll up. Be careful not to overstuff the wraps.

....

Variation:

Shrimp Caesar Salad Wrap: *Substitute 1 pound of peeled and deveined shrimp for the chicken. Grill or broil the shrimp for 1 to 2 minutes per side, or until just cooked through.*

....

Thai Chicken Salad Wrap

Dressing:

¼ cup peanut butter
2 tablespoons hoisin sauce
2 tablespoons reduced-sodium
    soy sauce
2 tablespoons reduced-sodium
    chicken broth
2 tablespoons honey
1 tablespoon dark sesame oil
1 tablespoon peeled and
    minced fresh ginger
1 teaspoon sugar
1 teaspoon Asian chili paste

4 boneless and skinless
    chicken breasts (about
    1½ pounds)
4 10- to 12-inch flour tortillas

Salad:

4 cups packed chopped
    lettuce
1 cup shredded carrots
1 cup chopped ripe tomatoes
    (optional)
½ cup shredded red cabbage
½ cup seeded and thinly
    sliced red bell peppers
½ cup coarsely chopped
    peanuts

Nowhere is the tortilla put to better use than in the making of giant wrapped sandwiches, known as "wraps." These flavorful sandwiches take the East-meets-West culinary concept to the next level: East not only meets West, but meets North and South as well. This Thai Chicken Salad Wrap, which teams crunchy greens and vegetables with grilled chicken and a sweet and spicy peanut sauce, is truly addictive. These flavors and textures will dance on your tongue, bring a big smile to your face, and leave you warm, happy, and well-fed. Save time by picking up some of these prepped veggies at your favorite salad bar.

Cooking Time: 30 minutes or less
Serves: 4

1. Preheat the broiler or grill.
2. Prepare the dressing: In a microwave-safe bowl, combine the peanut butter, hoisin sauce, soy sauce, broth, honey, sesame oil, ginger, sugar, and chili paste. Microwave for 30 seconds to 1 minute, or until warm and easy to mix. (You can also mix dressing in a food processor). Set aside.
3. Lightly brush the chicken with ¼ cup of the dressing. Broil or grill the chicken breasts, 4 to 5 minutes per side, or until cooked through. When cool, cut the chicken into thin strips and set aside.

4. If using a broiler, lower the heat to 350 degrees; if using a grill, reduce heat to low. Wrap the tortillas in aluminum foil and place in the oven or on the grill to warm for 10 minutes. (Tortillas can also be wrapped in a damp towel and warmed in the microwave on high for 15 to 30 seconds.)
5. Prepare the salad: In a large bowl, combine the lettuce, carrots, tomato, red cabbage, red peppers, and remaining dressing. Add the chicken and peanuts and toss again.
6. Assemble the wraps: Place 1 to 1½ cups of salad in the center of each tortilla. Tuck the bottom of the tortilla up over the filling, fold both sides of the tortilla toward the center, and roll up. Be careful not to over-stuff the wraps.

·················

Variation:

Thai Shrimp Salad Wrap: *Substitute 1 pound of peeled and deveined shrimp for the chicken. Grill or broil the shrimp for 1 to 2 minutes per side, or until just cooked through.*

·················

Chicken and Vegetables

4 boneless and skinless
    chicken breasts (about
    1½ pounds)
1 teaspoon salt
½ teaspoon ground black
    pepper
1 tablespoon olive oil
1 tablespoon butter
2 cups cleaned, julienned
    leeks (white part only)
2 cups small mushrooms,
    halved if large
2 cups quartered, sliced
    carrots (1-inch-thick
    pieces)
1 cup sliced celery (1-inch-
    thick pieces)
1 teaspoon minced garlic
1 teaspoon dried thyme
½ cup dry white wine or
    reduced-sodium
    chicken broth

This modern version of the classic French pot-au-feu, *or "chicken-in-a-pot," includes the classic vegetables but makes use of boneless chicken breasts for an extra-short cooking time. With such easy preparation and execution, this healthful low-fat dinner is destined to become a tradition in your home.*

Cooking Time: 60 minutes or less
Serves: 4

1. Sprinkle the chicken with salt and pepper.
2. In a large skillet over medium-high heat, add the oil and butter. Add the chicken and brown, 4 to 5 minutes per side. Remove the chicken and reserve.
3. Add the leeks, mushrooms, carrots, celery, and garlic and cook until softened, 5 to 8 minutes, stirring frequently.
4. Add the thyme and wine and stir to combine. Bring to a boil. Reduce the heat, cover, and simmer for 15 minutes.
5. Add the chicken, cover, and cook for 5 minutes, or until the chicken and vegetables are cooked through.

Chicken Chili

Chicken lovers rejoice! Here's a chili just for you. Using boneless chicken, this tasty treat cooks up quickly. Use different beans for variety—choose from white cannellini beans, black beans, or traditional pinto beans. Fresh jalapeños add some heat. Garnish with chopped cilantro, grated cheddar or Monterey Jack cheese, and avocado.

Cooking Time: 60 minutes or less
Serves: 4

1. In a large stock pot over medium heat, add the oil. Add the onions, red peppers, and jalapeños and sauté until softened, 5 to 8 minutes, stirring frequently.
2. Add the garlic and cook for 1 minute, stirring constantly.
3. Add the chicken and sauté until just cooked, 3 to 5 minutes.
4. Add the chili powder, cumin, oregano, salt, and cayenne pepper and stir to combine.
5. Add the broth and tomatoes and their juice. Bring to a boil.
6. Reduce the heat, cover, and simmer for 15 minutes, stirring occasionally.
7. Add the beans and simmer uncovered for 15 to 20 minutes, or until thickened and the flavors have melded, stirring occasionally.

2 tablespoons vegetable oil
1 cup coarsely chopped onions
½ cup seeded and coarsely chopped red bell peppers
2 tablespoons seeded and finely chopped fresh jalapeño peppers
2 teaspoons minced garlic
4 boneless and skinless chicken breasts or thighs, cut into 1-inch pieces (about 1½ pounds)
2 tablespoons chili powder
2 teaspoons ground cumin
1 teaspoon dried oregano
1 teaspoon salt
¼ teaspoon cayenne pepper (optional)
2 cups reduced-sodium chicken broth
1 14½-ounce can diced tomatoes
1 15¼-ounce can white beans, rinsed and drained
1 15¼-ounce can pinto beans, rinsed and drained

Mediterranean Chicken and Rice

1 teaspoon salt
½ teaspoon ground black
  pepper
4 boneless and skinless
  chicken breasts or
  thighs (about 1½
  pounds)
2 tablespoons olive oil
1 cup chopped onions
1 cup sliced mushrooms
1 tablespoon minced garlic
½ to 1 teaspoon red pepper
  flakes
1½ cups rice
½ cup dry white wine
2 cups reduced-sodium
  chicken broth
1 14½-ounce can diced
  tomatoes, drained, ½
  cup liquid reserved
2 tablespoons freshly
  squeezed lemon juice
2 tablespoons capers
¼ cup coarsely chopped green
  olives
½ cup coarsely chopped fresh
  basil (optional)

This delicious chicken and rice dish salutes the vibrant flavors of the Mediterranean. Typical of this region's style of cooking, the savory spices and vegetables—not a lot of fat or fillers—define and flavor the dish. Tangy lemon, capers, and olives mingle with a sublime mix of onions, mushrooms, garlic, and tomatoes for a harmonious mélange.

Cooking Time: 60 minutes or less
Serves: 4

1. Sprinkle the chicken with salt and pepper.
2. In a large skillet over medium-high heat, add the oil. Add the chicken and brown, 4 to 5 minutes per side. Remove the chicken and reserve.
3. Add the onions and mushrooms and sauté until softened, 5 to 8 minutes, stirring frequently.
4. Add the garlic and red pepper flakes and cook for 1 minute, stirring constantly.
5. Add the rice and stir to combine.
6. Add the wine, broth, and tomatoes and their reserved juice. Bring to a boil and stir to deglaze and dislodge any bits of food that have stuck to the bottom of the skillet.

7. Reduce the heat, cover, and simmer for 15 to 20 minutes, or until the rice is almost tender, stirring occasionally.

8. Add the lemon juice, capers, and olives and stir to combine. Add the reserved chicken, cover, and cook for 5 minutes, or until the chicken and rice are cooked through. Top with the basil.

· · · · · · · · · · · · · · · · ·

Variation:

Mediterranean Shrimp and Rice: *Substitute 1 pound of peeled and deveined shrimp for the chicken. Cook the shrimp for 1 to 2 minutes per side, or until just cooked through.*

· · · · · · · · · · · · · · · ·

Brunswick Stew

¼ cup all-purpose flour
1 tablespoon salt
½ teaspoon ground black
    pepper
¼ teaspoon cayenne pepper
1 3- to 4-pound chicken, cut
    into 8 pieces
3 tablespoons olive oil
2 cups chopped onions
¼ pound ham, thickly sliced
    and cut into ½-inch
    pieces
1½ cups peeled potatoes cut
    into ½-inch cubes
2 cups reduced-sodium
    chicken broth
1 14½-ounce can diced
    tomatoes, drained
1 tablespoon Worcestershire
    sauce
4 dashes Tabasco or other hot
    red pepper sauce
1 cup fresh or frozen corn
1 cup fresh or frozen lima
    beans

Lima beans, once relegated to under-the-table pass-offs to the family dog, are now back in vogue, gracing entrées in the most trend-setting restaurants. Back in their disparaged days, the most common place you'd find them was in this tasty smoky-flavored Southern standard.

Cooking Time: 60 minutes or less
Serves: 4

1. Combine the flour, salt, black pepper, and cayenne pepper. Coat the chicken with the seasoned flour, reserving any excess.
2. In a large skillet, over medium-high heat, add the oil. Add the chicken and brown, 3 to 5 minutes per side. Remove the chicken and reserve. (You may need to do this in two or more batches).
3. Discard all but 1 tablespoon of fat from the skillet. Reduce the heat to medium and add the onions. Cook until softened, 3 to 5 minutes. Add the ham and potatoes and sauté for 3 minutes, stirring frequently.
4. Add any reserved flour and stir until it is absorbed into the onions, 1 to 2 minutes.
5. Add the broth, tomatoes, Worcestershire sauce, and Tabasco. Bring to a boil and stir to deglaze and dislodge any bits of food that have stuck to the bottom of the skillet. Keep stirring until slightly thickened.

6. Return the chicken to the skillet. Reduce the heat, cover, and simmer for 30 minutes, basting with the cooking liquid and turning the chicken occasionally.
7. Add the corn and lima beans and simmer uncovered for 5 to 10 minutes, or until the chicken and vegetables are cooked through.

Spicy Pepper Chicken

1 3- to 4-pound chicken, cut into 8 pieces
1 tablespoon salt
1 teaspoon ground black pepper
3 tablespoons olive oil
2 cups coarsely chopped onions
3 cups sliced bell peppers (a mix of red, yellow, and orange)
2 tablespoons seeded and finely chopped fresh jalapeño peppers
1 tablespoon minced garlic
½ pound prosciutto, thickly sliced and cut into thin, 1-inch-long strips
1 28-ounce can diced tomatoes, drained
2 tablespoons coarsely chopped fresh basil, or 2 teaspoons dried
1 teaspoon orange zest (optional)

This French version of Chicken Cacciatore includes ingredients representative of the Basque region of Southwestern France—hot peppers, brightly colored bell peppers, garlic, and prosciutto. It's hearty enough to serve with a slab of crusty French bread, or you can try it over parsley rice or noodles coated with olive oil. Jalapeños vary in intensity, so use caution. When seeding or chopping hot chiles, wear rubber gloves to protect your hands from irritation. If you want more heat, add red pepper flakes before serving.

Cooking Time: 60 minutes or less
Serves: 4

1. Sprinkle the chicken with salt and pepper.
2. In a large skillet over medium-high heat, add the oil. Add the chicken and brown, 3 to 5 minutes per side. Remove the chicken and reserve. (You may need to do this in two or more batches).
3. Discard all but 1 tablespoon of fat from the skillet. Reduce the heat to medium and add the onions. Cook until softened, 3 to 5 minutes. Add the bell peppers, jalapeños, and garlic and cook for 5 minutes, stirring frequently.

4. Add the prosciutto, tomatoes, basil, and orange zest and stir to combine.

5. Return the chicken to the skillet. Reduce the heat, cover, and simmer for 30 to 40 minutes, or until the chicken and peppers are cooked through, basting with the cooking liquid and turning the chicken occasionally. If the sauce is too thin, remove the chicken and boil the sauce until it thickens.

Curried Chicken and Rice

1 3- to 4-pound chicken, cut
  into 8 pieces
1 tablespoon salt
½ teaspoon ground black
  pepper
3 tablespoons vegetable oil
2 cups chopped onions
2 teaspoons minced garlic
1 teaspoon peeled and minced
  fresh ginger
1½ cups basmati rice
3 tablespoons curry powder
1 teaspoon ground cumin
½ teaspoon red pepper flakes
3 cups reduced-sodium
  chicken broth
½ cup golden raisins
½ cup slivered almonds,
  lightly toasted

This fragrant and mild curry dish will please even the most timid eaters. Curry powder is actually a mixture of several spices, including cumin, coriander, fenugreek, red pepper, and turmeric. Its amalgamation was most likely a British invention, concocted by colonialists leaving the country who wanted to take a taste of India back home. In reality, curry powder is not representative of Indian cooking. There, different seasonings are combined for each dish and a standard curry blend is rarely, if ever, used. Because the spices in curry powder are ground, they tend to go stale; so for superior flavor, update your curry powder frequently. If basmati rice is unavailable, substitute your favorite variety.

Cooking Time: 60 minutes or less
Serves: 4

1. Preheat the oven to 375 degrees.
2. Sprinkle the chicken with salt and pepper.
3. In a large ovenproof skillet over medium-high heat, add the oil. Add the chicken and brown, 3 to 5 minutes per side. Remove the chicken and reserve. (You may need to do this in two or more batches).

4. Discard all but 1 tablespoon of fat from the skillet. Reduce the heat to medium and add the onions. Cook until softened, 3 to 5 minutes, stirring frequently.
5. Add the garlic and ginger and cook for 1 minute, stirring constantly.
6. Add the rice, curry powder, cumin, and red pepper flakes and stir to combine.
7. Add the broth. Bring to a boil, and stir to deglaze and dislodge any bits of food that have stuck to the bottom of the skillet.
8. Return the chicken to the skillet. Cover, place in the oven, and bake for 30 to 40 minutes, or until the rice is tender, the broth has been absorbed, and the chicken is cooked through.
9. Remove from the oven. Stir in the raisins and almonds.

Chicken Cacciatore

1 3- to 4-pound chicken, cut into 8 pieces
1 tablespoon salt
1 teaspoon ground black pepper
3 tablespoons olive oil
1 cup chopped onions
2 cups sliced bell peppers (a mix of red, yellow, orange, and/or green)
2 cups small mushrooms, quartered if large
2 teaspoons minced garlic
½ cup dry red wine
1 28-ounce can diced tomatoes, drained
1 teaspoon dried basil
½ teaspoon dried oregano
1 bay leaf

This robust Italian chicken braise is loaded with multicolored bell peppers, tomatoes, garlic, and mushrooms. While adding a salad and crusty bread makes this a complete meal, you could also serve it with pasta lightly tossed with capers in olive oil, or another Italian favorite, cornmeal polenta.

Cooking Time: 60 minutes or less
Serves: 4

1. Sprinkle the chicken with salt and pepper.
2. In a large skillet over medium-high heat, add the oil. Add the chicken and brown, 3 to 5 minutes per side. Remove the chicken and reserve. (You may need to do this in two or more batches).
3. Discard all but 1 tablespoon of fat from the skillet. Reduce the heat to medium and add the onions. Cook until softened, 3 to 5 minutes. Add the bell peppers, mushrooms, and garlic and cook for 5 minutes, stirring frequently.
4. Add the wine, tomatoes, basil, oregano, and bay leaf. Bring to a boil and stir to deglaze and dislodge any bits of food that have stuck to the bottom of the skillet.
5. Return the chicken to the skillet. Reduce the heat, cover, and simmer for 30 to 40 minutes, or until the chicken is cooked through, basting with the cooking liquid and turning the chicken occasionally. If the sauce is too thin, remove the chicken and boil the sauce until it thickens.

Chicken and Barley Stew

This healthful and flavorful stew combines an assortment of vegetables with barley, a nutritious grain that provides protein, niacin, thiamin, and potassium with very little sodium or fat. Studies have shown that this wonder grain also fights cholesterol production.

Cooking Time: 60 minutes or less
Serves: 4

2 tablespoons vegetable oil
1 cup coarsely chopped
    onions
1 cup coarsely chopped
    carrots
1 cup coarsely chopped celery
1 cup sliced mushrooms
2 teaspoons minced garlic
5 cups reduced-sodium
    chicken broth
1 cup drained canned diced
    tomatoes
1 cup pearl barley
1 pound boneless and skinless
    chicken breasts, cut
    into ½-inch pieces
1 teaspoon salt
½ teaspoon ground black
    pepper

1. In a large stock pot over medium-high heat, add the oil. Sauté the onions, carrots, celery, mushrooms, and garlic until softened, 5 to 8 minutes, stirring frequently.
2. Add the broth and tomatoes and stir to combine. Bring to a boil.
3. Add the barley and stir to combine.
4. Reduce the heat, cover, and simmer for 35 to 45 minutes, or until the barley is tender and the stew thickens, stirring occasionally.
5. Add the chicken and cook for 5 to 7 minutes, or until the chicken is cooked through. Season with salt and pepper.

Arroz con Pollo

1 3- to 4-pound chicken, cut into 8 pieces
1 tablespoon salt
½ teaspoon ground black pepper
3 tablespoons olive oil
1 cup chopped onions
1 cup seeded and chopped green bell peppers
1 cup seeded and chopped red bell peppers
1 teaspoon minced garlic
¼ pound ham, chopped (optional)
1½ cups rice
3 cups reduced-sodium chicken broth
1 teaspoon paprika
¼ teaspoon saffron (optional)
1 bay leaf
1 cup fresh or frozen peas
¼ cup pimentos (optional)

> The ubiquitous arroz con pollo, *Spanish for chicken and rice, is served all over the world, most notably in Spain, Cuba, and Latin America. This colorful dish's signature spice is saffron, which imparts its distinctive flavor and distinguishing yellow hue.*

Cooking Time: 60 minutes or less
Serves: 4

1. Preheat the oven to 375 degrees.
2. Sprinkle the chicken with salt and pepper.
3. In a large ovenproof skillet over medium-high heat, add the oil. Add the chicken and brown, 3 to 5 minutes per side. Remove the chicken and reserve. (You may need to do this in two or more batches).
4. Discard all but 1 tablespoon of fat from the skillet. Reduce the heat to medium and add the onions, both bell peppers, garlic, and ham. Cook until softened, 5 to 8 minutes, stirring frequently.
5. Add the rice and stir to combine.
6. Add the broth. Bring to a boil and stir to deglaze and dislodge any bits of food that have stuck to the bottom of the skillet.

7. Add the paprika, saffron, and bay leaf and stir to combine.
8. Return the chicken to the skillet. Cover, place in the oven, and bake for 30 minutes.
9. Stir in the peas and pimentos, cover, and bake for 5 to 10 minutes, or until the rice is tender, the broth has been absorbed, and the chicken is cooked through.

Creamy Dijon Chicken Stew

1 3- to 4-pound chicken, cut
    into 8 pieces
1 tablespoon salt
1 teaspoon ground black
    pepper
3 tablespoons olive oil
2 cups cleaned and thinly
    sliced leeks (white part
    only)
2 cups sliced carrots (½-inch-
    thick pieces)
1½ cups sliced new potatoes
10 large cloves garlic, peeled
3 tablespoons all-purpose flour
1½ cups reduced-sodium
    chicken broth
1 cup dry white wine
½ cup Dijon mustard
2 teaspoons dried tarragon or
    herbs de Provençe
    (optional)
¼ cup whipping cream
    (optional)

In this flavorful medley, chicken is sautéed with garlic, leeks, and vegetables and then simmered in a Dijon mustard–white wine sauce. This tasty condiment, a mild mustard paste blended with wine, is named for the city of Dijon in central France.

Cooking Time: 60 minutes or less
Serves: 4

1. Sprinkle the chicken with salt and pepper.
2. In a large skillet, over medium-high heat, add the oil. Add the chicken and brown, 3 to 5 minutes per side. Remove the chicken and reserve. (You may need to do this in two or more batches).
3. Discard all but 1 tablespoon of fat from the skillet. Reduce the heat to medium and add the leeks, carrots, potatoes, and garlic. Cook until softened, 3 to 5 minutes, stirring frequently.
4. Add the flour and cook for 1 to 2 minutes, stirring constantly.
5. Add the broth, wine, mustard, and tarragon. Bring to a boil and stir to deglaze and dislodge any bits of food that have stuck to the bottom of the skillet. Keep stirring until slightly thickened.

6. Return the chicken to the skillet. Reduce the heat, cover, and simmer for 30 to 40 minutes, or until the chicken is cooked through, basting with the cooking liquid and turning the chicken occasionally.
7. Remove the chicken and vegetables to the serving bowl using a slotted spoon and cover with foil. Add the cream and simmer until the liquid thickens, 2 to 3 minutes, stirring constantly. Pour the sauce over the chicken.

. . . .

Variation: *Although there is only a small amount of cream added, if you are watching your fat intake, or prefer a lighter dinner, omit the cream. If you omit the cream, boil the sauce until it thickens.*

. . . .

Turkey, Potatoes, Tomatoes, and Cheese

1 tablespoon olive oil
3 cups peeled and thinly sliced
     potatoes
2 tablespoons freshly
     squeezed lemon juice
2 teaspoons minced garlic
1 teaspoon salt
½ teaspoon ground black
     pepper
1 cup reduced-sodium
     chicken broth
4 boneless and skinless turkey
     breast fillets (about 1
     pound)
1 egg, beaten
2 cups bread crumbs,
     homemade or
     packaged
½ cup dry white wine
1 large ripe tomato, sliced
     (about ½ pound)
1 teaspoon dried oregano
1 teaspoon dried basil
½ pound mozzarella cheese,
     grated or shredded

This layered casserole pairs tender turkey fillets with thinly sliced potatoes, tomatoes, herbs, and cheese. Turkey cutlets tend to be thinner than chicken, so be careful not to overcook them. If substituting chicken, pound the fillets between waxed paper for uniform thickness.

Cooking Time: 60 minutes or less
Serves: 4

1. Preheat the oven to 450 degrees.
2. Lightly coat a 13 × 9 × 2-inch baking pan with the oil. Arrange the potatoes in slightly overlapping rows. Top with the lemon juice and sprinkle with the garlic, salt, and pepper. Add the broth.
3. Cover with aluminum foil and bake for 10 minutes. Uncover and bake for 10 to 20 minutes, or until the potatoes have begun to brown and cook through.
4. Meanwhile, dip the turkey breasts in the egg and press into the bread crumbs to coat. Set aside.
5. Remove the pan from the oven and reduce the heat to 400 degrees.
6. Place the turkey breasts on top of the potatoes. Drizzle with the wine. Top each fillet with tomato slices. Sprinkle the oregano and basil on top of the tomatoes. Top with the mozzarella cheese.
7. Bake for 10 to 15 minutes, or until the turkey has cooked through and the cheese has melted. For added browning, place under the broiler for 1 to 2 minutes.

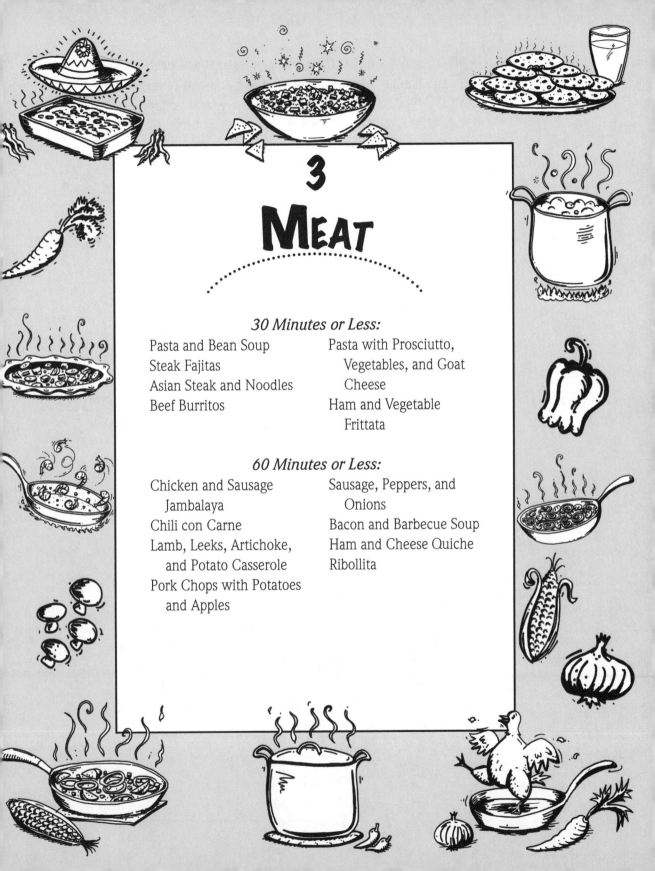

3

MEAT

30 Minutes or Less:

Pasta and Bean Soup
Steak Fajitas
Asian Steak and Noodles
Beef Burritos

Pasta with Prosciutto,
   Vegetables, and Goat
   Cheese
Ham and Vegetable
   Frittata

60 Minutes or Less:

Chicken and Sausage
   Jambalaya
Chili con Carne
Lamb, Leeks, Artichoke,
   and Potato Casserole
Pork Chops with Potatoes
   and Apples

Sausage, Peppers, and
   Onions
Bacon and Barbecue Soup
Ham and Cheese Quiche
Ribollita

From quick stir-fries to slowly simmered stews, beef, pork, and lamb are an important and exciting part of our diet. Although red meat was shunned a few years ago for being unhealthful, as a result of new breeding and feeding practices, beef is now lower in fat, calories, and cholesterol than ever before and pork is now bred to be almost a third leaner than a decade ago. Protein-rich red meat provides important nutrients, including niacin, B vitamins, iron, and zinc.

The best method for cooking meat is based on the muscle density of the cut. Because tender prime cuts of meat toughen if overcooked, lean steaks are best when quickly grilled or combined with vegetables in simple sautés. The more muscled and fattier cuts are best adapted to long, slow cooking, which tenderizes and coaxes the flavor from every sinewy strand—and makes it impossible to prepare a meat stew in under an hour or two. While this is bad news for days when quick meals are needed, it is a wonderful and luxurious method of cooking for entertaining. Stews can be put up to simmer long before guests are due, allowing the time before company arrives to be stress-free.

Beef Tips:

- If you are unfamiliar with different cuts of meat, seek advice from a knowledgeable butcher. You can usually find meat-cutters in your local supermarket willing to share their wisdom.
- Check with your butcher before buying generically labeled "stew meat." It may actually be a leaner cut of meat packaged to look more appealing but will toughen with extended cooking. It is often more economical to cut your own stew meat from a larger piece of meat. If you do, be sure to account for added waste and bone weight when figuring out how much to buy.

- When buying beef, search for meat that is bright red. Look for marbling—flecks of fat within the meat. We are all "fat conscious" today, but we mustn't discount fat's benefits: added flavor, tenderness, and juiciness.

- Pork should be pink to pale red, not crimson. Avoid pork with blood or discoloration in the meat. When choosing prepared meats like ham or prosciutto, sample different quality brands to find the one you like best.

- We have become increasingly aware of bacterial contamination of meat. *E. coli* is the pathogen most commonly associated with raw beef. Before using meats, cut off excess fat and rinse with cold water (making sure it doesn't spray all over the counters). After cutting meat, always thoroughly wash your hands, counters, cutting boards, and knives with warm, soapy water. Store uncooked meat separately from other ingredients to prevent cross-contamination. These bacteria are killed with proper cooking. Never eat raw meat.

- Always check the expiration date before buying packaged meat, and store it in your refrigerator. If you are unable to use meat within three days or by its expiration date, it is best to freeze it. To prevent bacterial growth, always thaw meat in your refrigerator or microwave, not at room temperature.

- If you find you have more meat than you need for your meal, wrap, label, and store the extra in the freezer.

- For better browning, always pat the meat dry with paper towels before searing. Searing caramelizes the surface of the meat, adding flavor. When searing meat, don't overcrowd the pan or the meat will steam rather than brown, giving it an unappealing gray hue.

- When cutting meat for sautéing, slice against the grain for added tenderness.

- Use uniformly sized pieces of meat for more consistent cooking times.
- Meat stews should be cooked at a slow simmer, not a boil, to fully develop their character and flavor.
- Before serving stews, use a soup spoon or paper towels to skim off any fat or froth that has risen to the surface or run an ice cube over the surface to quickly solidify any liquid fat. If you are cooking and refrigerating the stew, the fat will harden when chilled and is easily removed.
- Most meat stews improve overnight and are even better reheated.
- Add leftover meat to vegetarian entrées for extra protein.

Pasta and Bean Soup

This classic Italian soup, known as pasta e fagioli *or* zuppa di fagioli, *came to worldwide attention with the song "That's Amore" in the movie* Moonstruck. *This tomato-based soup is studded with pasta, white beans, and pancetta—rolled Italian bacon. It's the perfect meal on a chilly night, served with toasted slices of Italian bread rubbed with garlic and drizzled with olive oil and a big green salad full of crunchy fennel.*

1 tablespoon olive oil
¼ pound pancetta or prosciutto, chopped
1 cup finely chopped onions
¼ cup finely chopped celery
2 teaspoons minced garlic
1 teaspoon dried rosemary
6 cups reduced-sodium chicken broth
1 14½-ounce can diced tomatoes, drained
1½ cups small pasta shapes
1 15-ounce can cannellini or white beans, rinsed and drained
2 cups escarole, Swiss chard, or spinach leaves (optional)
⅓ cup grated Parmesan cheese (optional)

Cooking Time: 30 minutes or less
Serves: 4

1. In a large stock pot over medium heat, add the oil. Sauté the pancetta for 8 to 10 minutes, or until lightly browned, stirring frequently.
2. Add the onions and celery and cook until softened, 3 to 5 minutes.
3. Add the garlic and rosemary and cook for 1 minute, stirring constantly.
4. Add the broth and tomatoes. Bring to a boil.
5. Add the pasta and cook for 5 to 8 minutes, or until almost tender, stirring occasionally.
6. Add the beans and escarole. Reduce the heat and simmer for 5 minutes. Season with salt and pepper to taste. Top each serving with the Parmesan cheese.

Steak Fajitas

¼ cup freshly squeezed lime
    juice
2 tablespoons olive oil
1 tablespoon minced garlic
1 teaspoon salt
1 teaspoon chili powder
1 pound top sirloin, thinly
    sliced
8 8- to 10-inch flour tortillas
2 tablespoons vegetable oil
1 large yellow onion, peeled
    and sliced (about ¾
    pound)
1 large red onion, peeled and
    sliced (about ¾ pound)
1 large red bell pepper, seeded
    and sliced (about ½
    pound)
1 large green bell pepper
    seeded and sliced
    (about ½ pound)
2 cups guacamole
¼ pound cheddar cheese,
    grated or shredded
1 cup tomato salsa
1 cup sour cream
1 cup rinsed and drained
    canned black beans

Fajitas are a fabulous party dish. They are simple to prepare and guests can roll up their sleeves and lend a helping hand. Marinated steak, bell peppers, and onions are wrapped in warmed tortillas and served with a variety of accompaniments— salsa, guacamole, black beans, sour cream, and grated cheddar cheese—so people can customize their fillings. The steak, onions, and peppers can also all be grilled on the barbecue for extra flavor.

Cooking Time: 30 minutes or less
Serves: 4

1. In a large baking pan or zip-top bag, combine the lime juice, olive oil, garlic, salt, chili powder, and steak. Marinate for at least 30 minutes, or up to 24 hours in the refrigerator.
2. Preheat the oven to 350 degrees.
3. Wrap the tortillas in aluminum foil and place in the oven to warm for 10 minutes. (Tortillas can also be wrapped in a damp towel and warmed in the microwave on high for 15 to 30 seconds).
4. In a large skillet over medium-high heat, add the vegetable oil. Sauté both onions for 3 to 5 minutes, stirring frequently. Add both bell peppers and cook for 5 to 8 minutes, until crisp-tender. Remove the vegetables and reserve.

5. Drain the marinade from the meat. Add the steak and sauté for 3 minutes. Return the vegetables to the skillet and stir to combine.

6. Serve the meat and vegetables with the tortillas, guacamole, cheese, salsa, sour cream, and black beans.

· · · · · · · · · · · · · · · · ·

Variations:

Shrimp Fajitas: *Substitute 1 pound of large peeled and deveined shrimp for the steak. Marinate the shrimp for 30 minutes. Cook for 1 to 2 minutes per side, or until just cooked through.*

Fish Fajitas: *Substitute 1 pound of thinly sliced mahi-mahi, swordfish, or wahoo for the steak. Marinate the fish for 30 minutes. Cook for 1 to 3 minutes per side, or until just cooked through.*

Chicken Fajitas: *Substitute 1 pound of thinly sliced boneless and skinless chicken breasts for the steak. Marinate the chicken for 30 minutes to 1 hour. Cook for 3 to 5 minutes per side, or until cooked through.*

· · · · · · · · · · · · · · · · ·

Asian Steak and Noodles

2 tablespoons vegetable oil
1 pound top sirloin, thinly
  sliced
2 3-ounce packages "Oriental"
  flavor instant ramen
  noodles, broken up
  into small pieces
2 cups broccoli florets, halved
  if large
1 cup thinly sliced carrots, cut
  diagonally
1 cup thinly sliced mushrooms
½ cup seeded and thinly
  sliced red bell peppers
2 cups water
½ teaspoon ground ginger
1 cup snow pea pods
½ cup sliced water chestnuts
½ cup fresh or frozen peas
2 tablespoons thinly sliced
  scallions

This Asian-flavored beef dish uses packaged instant ramen noodles. With the aid of this convenience, you can have a complete dinner on the table, packed with tender steak, vibrant veggies, and highly flavored noodles in under thirty minutes. This dish is also tasty with sliced boneless and skinless chicken breasts or large shrimp.

Cooking Time: 30 minutes or less
Serves: 4

1. In a large skillet over medium-high heat, add the oil. Cook the beef for 3 minutes. Remove the meat and toss with 1 seasoning packet from the noodles. Set aside.
2. Add the broccoli, carrots, mushrooms, and red peppers and sauté until almost cooked through, 8 to 10 minutes, stirring frequently.
3. Add the water, ginger, noodles, and remaining seasoning packet and stir to combine. Bring to a boil.
4. Add the snow pea pods, water chestnuts, and peas. Reduce the heat and simmer for 5 to 8 minutes, or until the noodles are tender, stirring occasionally.
5. Add the beef and scallions and stir to combine. Cook for 1 minute.

. . . .

Variations:

Asian Chicken and Noodles: *Substitute 1 pound of thinly sliced boneless and skinless chicken breasts for the steak. Cook the chicken for 3 to 5 minutes, or until cooked through.*

Asian Shrimp and Noodles: *Substitute 1 pound of large peeled and deveined shrimp for the steak. Cook the shrimp for 1 to 2 minutes per side, or until just cooked through.*

. . . .

Beef Burritos

4 10- to 12-inch flour tortillas
1 tablespoon vegetable oil
1 cup finely chopped onions
1¼ pounds lean ground beef
1 tablespoon chili powder
1 teaspoon ground cumin
1 teaspoon salt
3 cups coarsely chopped
      spinach leaves
      (optional)
1¼ cups chunky tomato salsa
1 cup fresh or frozen corn
¼ pound cheddar cheese,
      grated or shredded

In this south-of-the-border treat, lean ground beef, vegetables, and tasty seasonings are tossed in a skillet and then wrapped in warm tortillas. It's a fast, easy, and inexpensive family meal that will be on your table in less than thirty minutes. More important, it helps disguise vegetables from children who fear anything healthful! Have lots of toppings handy. Extra salsa, sour cream, shredded lettuce, chopped tomatoes, and guacamole all make great add-ons.

Cooking Time: 30 minutes or less
Serves: 4

1. Preheat the oven to 350 degrees.
2. Wrap the tortillas in aluminum foil and place in the oven to warm for 10 minutes. (Tortillas can also be wrapped in a damp towel and warmed in the microwave on high for 15 to 30 seconds).
3. In a large skillet over medium-high heat, add the oil. Add the onions and cook until softened, 3 to 5 minutes, stirring frequently.
4. Add the beef, chili powder, cumin, and salt. Cook, breaking up the meat, until the beef is no longer pink, 8 to 10 minutes, stirring frequently. Drain any excess fat from the skillet.

Meat

5. Add the spinach, salsa, and corn and cook until heated through, 3 to 5 minutes. Remove from the heat and stir in the cheese.

6. Spoon one-quarter of the beef into the center of each tortilla and add any toppings. Tuck the bottom of the tortilla up over the filling, fold both sides of the tortilla toward the center, and roll up. Be careful not to over-stuff the burrito.

·················

Variation:

Turkey Burritos: *Substitute 1¼ pounds of ground turkey for the beef.*

·················

Pasta with Prosciutto, Vegetables, and Goat Cheese

½ cup drained and coarsely
   chopped oil-packed
   sun-dried tomatoes
¼ cup olive oil
¼ pound prosciutto, ham, or
   salami, thinly sliced
¼ teaspoon red pepper flakes
2 cloves garlic, peeled
2 cups broccoli florets, halved
   if large
¾ pound spaghetti or other
   pasta
1 cup fresh or frozen peas
½ cup thinly sliced fresh basil
¼ pound goat cheese,
   crumbled
1 teaspoon salt
½ teaspoon ground black
   pepper
¼ cup grated Parmesan
   cheese

This colorful dish teams emerald broccoli, peas, and basil with crimson sun-dried tomatoes, strips of rosy prosciutto, steaming pasta, and creamy goat cheese. Delicious, healthful, and filling, it's a winning trifecta for cooks in a hurry. When cooking both the vegetables and the pasta in the same pot, it is helpful to have a pasta set with a removable insert. Otherwise, a strainer with a long handle will do.

Cooking Time: 30 minutes or less
Serves: 4

1. In the serving bowl, combine the sun-dried tomatoes, oil, prosciutto, and red pepper flakes. Set aside.
2. In a large pot over high heat, put the water up to boil for the pasta.
3. When the water is boiling, blanch the garlic for 30 to 45 seconds. (For easy blanching, skewer the garlic or use a mesh spoon to scoop it out). Rinse the garlic under cold water, pat dry, mince, and add to the serving bowl.
4. Add the broccoli and cook for 3 to 4 minutes, or until crisp-tender. Remove to the serving bowl.
5. Add the pasta and cook for 7 minutes. Add the peas and cook for 1 to 2 minutes, or until the pasta is al dente. Drain, reserving 2 to 3 tablespoons of pasta water.

6. Combine the pasta, reserved pasta water, basil, goat cheese, salt, and pepper with the sun-dried tomato mixture and stir to combine. Top with the Parmesan cheese.

· · · · · · · · · · · · · · · ·

Variation:

Pasta with Shrimp, Prosciutto, Vegetables, and Goat Cheese: *Add ¾ pound of peeled and deveined shrimp in step 5 before adding the pasta. Cook the shrimp for 1 to 2 minutes, or until just cooked through. Remove to the serving bowl.*

Pasta with Vegetables and Goat Cheese: *For a vegetarian dish, omit the prosciutto.*

· · · · · · · · · · · · · · · ·

Ham and Vegetable Frittata

1 tablespoon butter
½ cup coarsely chopped
    mushrooms
¼ cup finely chopped red
    onions
¼ cup seeded and finely
    chopped green or red
    bell peppers
8 eggs
¼ pound ham, chopped
2 ounces Swiss cheese, grated,
    or 2 ounces brie, sliced
    into 1-inch pieces
½ teaspoon salt
¼ teaspoon ground black
    pepper

After years of hard knocks, eggs are finally receiving the nutritional recognition they deserve. In addition to being an inexpensive source of protein, eggs are especially attractive for hurried cooks because they are quickly prepared. This light dinner, reminiscent of the classic American "Western omelet," adapts perfectly to the ease of frittata cooking. Substitute any vegetables or seasonings to make it your own creation. I highly recommend using a nonstick pan, which allows you to move the frittata easily during cooking.

Cooking Time: 30 minutes or less
Serves: 4

1. Preheat the oven to 350 degrees.
2. In a 10- or 11-inch nonstick, ovenproof skillet over medium-high heat, add the butter. Sauté the mushrooms, onions, and bell peppers until softened, 3 to 5 minutes, stirring frequently.
3. Meanwhile, in a medium bowl, beat the eggs. Add the ham, cheese, salt, and pepper.
4. Reduce the heat to medium. Pour the eggs on top of the vegetables. Cook without stirring for 1 minute, or until the eggs are almost set on the bottom. Continue cooking, using a spatula to lift the edges of the frittata toward the center of the skillet, while gently tilting the pan so the uncooked eggs run underneath the bot-

tom of the frittata. Cook for 30 to 40 seconds and repeat the process several times until the egg on top is still wet, but not runny.

5. Place in the oven. Bake for 3 to 7 minutes, or until the top is just set. Do not overcook.

6. Remove from the oven, run a spatula around the skillet edge to loosen the frittata, and slide or invert it onto a serving plate.

Chicken and Sausage Jambalaya

1 2- to 2½-pound chicken, cut into 8 pieces
1 tablespoon salt
1 teaspoon ground black pepper
3 tablespoons vegetable oil
1 cup chopped onions
1 cup seeded and chopped green bell peppers
2 teaspoons minced garlic
1 14½-ounce can diced tomatoes, drained
½ pound smoked andouille sausage, or Louisiana smoked sausage, or kielbasa, halved lengthwise and sliced ½-inch thick
1 teaspoon dried thyme
¼ teaspoon cayenne pepper
1 bay leaf
3 cups reduced-sodium chicken broth
1½ cups rice

*Jambalaya is as much a part of New Orleans as Mardi Gras and Zydeco music. The name for this spicy Cajun–Creole dish is derived from two French words—*jambon* for ham and* a là *for on top of—and the African word for rice,* ya. *Like much of Cajun cooking, it makes the most of ingredients found on hand—and there are as many variations of jambalaya as there are bars on Bourbon Street. This version features chicken and sausage, but ham and shrimp are two other popular additions.*

Cooking Time: 60 minutes or less
Serves: 4

1. Sprinkle the chicken with salt and pepper.
2. In a large skillet over medium-high heat, add the oil. Add the chicken and brown, 3 to 5 minutes per side. Remove the chicken and reserve. (You may need to do this in two or more batches).
3. Discard all but 1 tablespoon of the fat from the skillet. Reduce the heat to medium and add the onions, green peppers, and garlic. Cook until softened, 5 to 8 minutes, stirring frequently.

4. Add the tomatoes, sausage, thyme, cayenne pepper, and bay leaf and stir to combine.
5. Add the broth. Bring to a boil and stir to deglaze and dislodge any bits of food that have stuck to the bottom of the skillet.
6. Add the rice and stir to combine.
7. Return the chicken to the skillet. Reduce the heat, cover, and simmer for 30 to 40 minutes, or until the rice is tender, the broth has been absorbed, and the chicken is cooked through, stirring occasionally.

Chili con Carne

2 tablespoons vegetable oil
1 cup coarsely chopped
   onions
1 cup seeded and coarsely
   chopped green bell
   peppers
2 teaspoons minced garlic
1½ pounds lean ground beef
2 cups canned crushed
   tomatoes
2 cups reduced-sodium beef
   broth
3 tablespoons chili powder
1 teaspoon ground cumin
1 teaspoon salt
½ teaspoon cayenne pepper
½ teaspoon dried oregano
1 15¼-ounce can kidney
   beans, rinsed and
   drained

Contrary to popular belief, Chili con Carne is an American invention, not an import from south of the border. Texans lay claim to its origin, but its true beginnings are undocumented. What is well known is its overwhelming popularity, as evidenced by the number of festivals held in its honor, the monumental number of recipe variations, and the worshipping of its heat and spice by "chili-heads" all over the world. This classic meat and bean chili is the quintessential party fare. It's a snap to prepare, and the recipe can easily be doubled or tripled to accommodate a crowd of hungry eaters. You can vary the seasonings to make it as potent as you want. If you like your chili super hot, add some extra cayenne pepper, jalapeño peppers, or Tabasco. Make sure you have lots of toppings on hand: sour cream, grated cheddar cheese, chopped red onions, cilantro, ripe tomatoes, and lime are all naturals. Serve with a big salad and cornbread or tortilla chips, and it's a party.

Cooking Time: 60 minutes or less
Serves: 4

1. In a large stock pot over medium heat, add the oil. Add the onions and green peppers and sauté until softened, 3 to 5 minutes, stirring frequently.

2. Add the garlic and cook for 1 minute, stirring constantly.
3. Add the ground beef and cook for 5 to 8 minutes, or until just cooked through, using a fork or spatula to break up the meat into small pieces.
4. Add the tomatoes, broth, chili powder, cumin, salt, cayenne pepper, and oregano and stir to combine. Bring to a boil.
5. Add the kidney beans. Reduce the heat and simmer for 45 minutes, or until thickened and the flavors have melded, stirring occasionally.

· · · · · · · · · · · · · · · ·

Variation:

Turkey Chili: *Substitute ground turkey for the beef.*

· · · · · · · · · · · · · · · ·

Lamb, Leek, Artichoke, and Potato Casserole

8 1-inch-thick lamb chops, trimmed of excess fat (about 2½ pounds)
1 tablespoon minced garlic
2 tablespoons olive oil
3 cups cleaned, julienned leeks (white part only)
6 cups peeled and thinly sliced potatoes
1 teaspoon dried thyme
1 teaspoon salt
½ teaspoon ground black pepper
1 cup reduced-sodium chicken broth
2 cups frozen or canned artichoke hearts, halved

Tender lamb chops are paired with flavorful leeks and smothered with potatoes and artichoke hearts in this easy stove-to-oven casserole. Leeks, a milder member of the onion family, resemble giant scallions. When sautéed, they impart a delicate and sweet flavor that enhances whatever they are cooked with.

Cooking Time: 60 minutes or less
Serves: 4

1. Preheat the oven to 425 degrees.
2. Rub the lamb chops with the garlic.
3. In a large ovenproof skillet over medium-high heat, add the oil. Add the lamb chops and brown, 2 minutes per side. (You may need to do this in two or more batches). Remove the lamb and reserve.
4. Add the leeks and sauté until softened, 3 to 5 minutes, stirring frequently.
5. Add the potatoes, thyme, salt, and pepper and stir to combine.
6. Add the broth. Bring to a boil.
7. Add the lamb and artichokes to the skillet, cover, and place in the oven. Bake for 10 to 15 minutes. Uncover, baste with the cooking liquid, and bake for 10 to 15 minutes, or until the lamb and potatoes are cooked through.

Pork Chops with Potatoes and Apples

In this autumnal dish, delicately seasoned pork is a natural match for apples and potatoes. Pork, once maligned as high in fat, is now bred to be much leaner. In fact, it now has 50 percent less fat than it did twenty years ago. So enjoy "the other white meat" in this delicious stove-to-oven meal.

Cooking Time: 60 minutes or less
Serves: 4

1. Preheat the oven to 425 degrees.
2. Sprinkle the pork chops with the salt, thyme, sage, and pepper.
3. In a large ovenproof skillet over medium-high heat, add the butter. Add the pork chops and brown, 2 minutes per side. Remove the pork and reserve.
4. Add the onions and sauté until softened, 3 to 5 minutes, stirring frequently.
5. Stir in the mustard. Top with the potatoes, apples, broth, and apple juice and stir to combine. Bring to a boil.
6. Cover, place in the oven, and bake for 10 minutes. Uncover, stir, and bake for 10 to 15 minutes, or until the potatoes are tender.
7. Return the pork to the skillet, cover, and bake for 7 to 12 minutes, or until the pork is cooked through.

4 1-inch-thick boneless pork chops, trimmed of excess fat (about 1½ to 2 pounds)
1 teaspoon salt
1 teaspoon dried thyme
1 teaspoon dried sage
½ teaspoon ground black pepper
2 tablespoons butter
1 cup chopped onions
2 teaspoons Dijon mustard
4 cups peeled and thinly sliced potatoes
4 cups peeled, cored, and thinly sliced Granny Smith apples
½ cup reduced-sodium chicken broth
½ cup apple juice or cider

Sausage, Peppers, and Onions

2 tablespoons olive oil
1½ pounds hot or sweet
    Italian sausage, sliced
    1½ inches thick
1 large yellow onion, peeled
    and sliced ½ inch thick
    (about ¾ pound)
2 large bell peppers (red,
    yellow, orange, and/or
    green), sliced ½ inch
    thick (about 1 pound)
1 tablespoon minced garlic
1 28-ounce can Italian plum
    tomatoes
½ cup dry red wine
2 teaspoons dried oregano
1 teaspoon dried basil
1 teaspoon fennel seeds
    (optional)
¼ teaspoon red pepper flakes
1 teaspoon salt
½ teaspoon ground black
    pepper

For me, the aromatic and tasty combination of sausage, peppers, and onions always stirs memories of strolling by Fenway Park, the great Boston baseball field. There, food vendors lined the streets leading up to the stadium, filling historic Kenmore Square with tempting aromas, none more intoxicating than this winning combination. Whether the Red Sox won or lost, if a sausage sandwich was enjoyed, the evening was not a total disappointment. Make sure to serve crusty rolls on the side.

Cooking Time: 60 minutes or less
Serves: 4

1. In a large skillet over medium-high heat, add the oil. Add the sausage and brown on all sides, 8 to 10 minutes. (You may need to do this in two or more batches). Remove the sausage and reserve.
2. Discard all but 1 tablespoon of fat from the skillet. Reduce the heat to medium and add the onions. Cook until softened, 3 to 5 minutes. Add the bell peppers and garlic and cook for 5 minutes, stirring frequently.
3. Add the tomatoes and their juice, wine, oregano, basil, fennel seeds, and red pepper flakes and stir to combine and to break up any large pieces of tomato.

Bring to a boil and stir to deglaze and dislodge any bits of food that have stuck to the bottom of the skillet.

4. Return the sausage to the skillet. Reduce the heat, cover, and simmer for 30 minutes, stirring occasionally. Season with salt and pepper.

••••••••••••••••

Variation:

Turkey Sausage, Onions, and Peppers: *Substitute turkey or chicken sausage for the Italian sausage.*

••••••••••••••••

Bacon and Barbecue Soup

½ pound bacon, cut into 2-inch pieces
2 cups sliced mushrooms
1 cup coarsely chopped onions
3½ cups reduced-sodium chicken broth
1 28-ounce can diced tomatoes
1 15-ounce can tomato sauce
¼ cup barbecue sauce
2 tablespoons red wine vinegar
1 tablespoon coarsely chopped fresh Italian parsley (optional)
1 teaspoon chili powder
1 teaspoon salt
½ teaspoon ground black pepper
2 cups medium-sized shell noodles or other pasta shape

This soup was created by George V. Jackson at the age of eight. Jackson, as he is known to friends and family, learned to fend for himself in the kitchen at an early age. Now fifty years have passed and time hasn't altered his recipe. Although Jackson calls his creation "vinegar soup," his grandsons, for whom he now cooks, refer to it as "Grandpa's Bacon Soup" when asking for seconds. Because the barbecue sauce adds such a distinctive flavor, I call it Bacon and Barbecue Soup.

Cooking Time: 60 minutes or less
Serves: 4

1. In a large stock pot over medium heat, sauté the bacon until cooked but not crisp, 6 to 8 minutes, stirring frequently.
2. Discard all but 1 tablespoon of fat from the skillet. Add the mushrooms and onions and cook until softened, 5 to 8 minutes, stirring frequently.
3. Add the broth, tomatoes and their juice, tomato sauce, barbecue sauce, vinegar, parsley, chili powder, salt, and pepper and stir to combine. Bring to a boil.

4. Reduce the heat, partially cover, and simmer for 30 minutes, stirring occasionally.
5. Bring to a boil and add the noodles. Stir to combine. Cook for 7 to 11 minutes, or until the noodles are cooked through, stirring occasionally. This soup will thicken as it stands. If necessary, add extra broth or water to achieve the desired consistency.

Ham and Cheese Quiche

Crust:

1¼ cups all-purpose flour
¼ teaspoon salt
½ cup (1 stick) unsalted
    butter, chilled and cut
    into ½-inch pieces
2 to 4 tablespoons ice water

Filling:

4 eggs
1 cup cream or milk
1 cup milk
½ teaspoon salt
¼ teaspoon ground black
    pepper
½ pound ham, chopped
¼ cup finely chopped red
    onions
5 ounces Swiss cheese, grated
    or shredded

Contrary to popular belief, real men do eat quiche . . . and what's more, they usually ask for seconds. Quiche has a real place in a busy household. It can be prepared in minutes and be on the table within the hour. Served with a salad loaded with crispy vegetables, this classic meal will never go out of style. Make your own crust or buy a pre-made crust and fit it into a 9-inch pie plate.

Cooking Time: 60 minutes or less
Serves: 4

1. Prepare the crust: In a food processor fitted with a metal chopping blade, mix the flour and salt (5 seconds). Add the butter and pulse until the mixture resembles coarse meal (10 short pulses). Sprinkle the minimum amount of water over the mixture and pulse until distributed throughout the dough and the crumbs start sticking together (5 to 10 pulses). Process just until the dough holds together, adding the remaining water if necessary. Do not allow the dough to form a ball.
2. Scrape the dough onto the work surface. Shape the dough into a 1-inch-thick disc. Wrap the dough tightly with plastic wrap and refrigerate for 30 minutes, or until it is firm enough to roll out.
3. Preheat the oven to 450 degrees.

4. Roll out the dough and fit into a 9-inch pie pan. Prick the dough with a fork and bake for 5 to 10 minutes, or until lightly browned. Remove from the oven and reduce the temperature to 350 degrees.

5. Prepare the filling: Meanwhile, in a medium bowl, beat the eggs, cream, milk, salt, and pepper. Add the ham and onions and stir to combine. Set aside.

6. Line the partially baked pie crust with the cheese. Add the egg mixture.

7. Bake for 40 to 50 minutes, or until the eggs are set and the center doesn't jiggle. If the crust begins to brown before the quiche is ready, cover it with aluminum foil to prevent burning. Let stand 5 to 10 minutes before serving.

Ribollita

2 tablespoons olive oil
¼ pound pancetta or
    prosciutto, chopped
1 cup chopped onions
1 cup thinly sliced leeks
    (white part only)
½ cup coarsely chopped
    carrots
½ cup coarsely chopped celery
2 teaspoons minced garlic
½ head Savoy cabbage, thinly
    sliced
6 cups reduced-sodium
    chicken broth
1 14½-ounce can diced
    tomatoes
1 cup rinsed and drained
    canned cannellini or
    small white beans
¼ cup coarsely chopped fresh
    basil
1 teaspoon salt
½ teaspoon ground black
    pepper
2 cups 1-inch cubed stale
    crusty sourdough,
    French, or Italian
    bread
½ cup grated Parmesan
    cheese

This peasant-style bread and vegetable soup is a mainstay of Tuscan dining. Ribollita, which means "reboiled," originated in the days when cooks traditionally stretched out their minestrone soup for a second serving by adding leftover bread. It is much debated whether Ribollita is best enjoyed right after cooking in its more liquid state, or if it is even better after standing or reheating, when the bread expands and the soup takes on a thick porridge-like consistency.

Cooking Time: 60 minutes or less
Serves: 4

1. Heat the oil in a large stock pot. Sauté the pancetta over medium heat for 8 to 10 minutes, or until lightly browned, stirring frequently.
2. Add the onions, leeks, carrots, celery, and garlic and cook until softened, 5 to 8 minutes, stirring occasionally.
3. Add the cabbage and cook for 2 to 3 minutes, stirring constantly.
4. Add the broth and tomatoes and their juice. Bring to a boil.
5. Add the beans, basil, salt, and pepper. Reduce the heat and simmer for 20 minutes, stirring occasionally.
6. Add the bread and cook for 5 minutes. Top each serving with the Parmesan cheese.

4

SEAFOOD

30 Minutes or Less:

Oriental Shrimp and
  Vegetable Pasta
Shrimp and Asparagus
  Risotto
Beer-Battered Fish Tacos
Seafood Stew
Coconut Fish and Shrimp
  Stew

Spicy Shrimp with Dried-
  Fruit Pilaf
Shrimp and Feta Cheese
Thai Shrimp and Jasmine
  Rice
Shrimp and White Bean
  Stew
Thai Shrimp and Cello-
  phane Noodles

60 Minutes or Less:

Oven-Baked Fish with
  Roasted Vegetables
Bouillabaisse
Shrimp and Sausage
  Gumbo
Paella

Manhattan Clam
  Chowder
New England Clam and
  Fish Chowder
Smoked Salmon and Goat
  Cheese Quiche
Cioppino

We have not always been a piscivorous nation. But as we become more health conscious, seafood is playing a bigger role in our diet. While many of us grew up associating seafood with soggy fish sticks and smelly kitchens, we now have to revise our perceptions. With so many varieties of seafood widely available, and newly perfected "quick" cooking techniques like grilling and stir-frying, fried and breaded is no longer the only option. Now fish is no longer cooked to a rubbery death, and we can celebrate its moist, firm texture and superior flavor.

Seafood is gracing our dinner tables with greater regularity—and for good reason. Seafood is high in protein and low in calories and saturated fats. It provides B vitamins, phosphorus, potassium, iron, zinc, calcium, iodine, and omega-3 fatty acids. These acids reduce blood clots, prevent heart disease, and lower cholesterol. In addition to its great nutritional value, seafood is quick cooking and requires very little added fat for its preparation.

In this chapter, you'll find fast and temptingly easy shrimp recipes and a variety of full-flavored seafood stews, stirfries, and soups.

A word of warning: Seafood, especially shellfish, can be quite pricey, but there are many ways around this. Most recipes allow a lot of flexibility when selecting fish. Inexpensive mussels are easily substituted when clams are costly, and several options are given for fish fillets so you can take advantage of whichever one is on sale. Splurge for special occasions and conserve on others.

Seafood Tips:

- Unfortunately, specialty fish markets are becoming a thing of the past. To offset this, supermarket fish departments are offering greater variety and are becoming more knowledgeable about different types of fish. Check out different markets to see which has the best quality, variety, and price.

- Buy fresh fish rather than frozen or previously frozen whenever possible. The exception is shrimp, which has almost always been previously frozen.
- Seafood should smell clean and sweet. It should never smell "fishy" or have an unpleasant or ammonia-like odor. Fish should look firm, moist, and translucent. Avoid slimy, dried-out, or discolored fish. Mussels, clams, and oysters should be alive, clean, free of debris, and have tightly closed, intact shells.
- Store seafood in your refrigerator. It is best to consume fish within twenty-four to thirty-six hours of its purchase. Always thaw and marinate seafood in the refrigerator, not at room temperature, to prevent bacterial growth.
- Before using seafood, rinse it with cold water (making sure it doesn't spray all over the counters) to remove surface bacteria. After cutting seafood, always thoroughly wash your hands, counters, cutting boards, and knives with warm, soapy water. Store uncooked seafood separately from other ingredients to prevent cross-contamination.
- When cooking clams, oysters, or mussels in their shells, always discard any that do not open. Unopened shells most likely mean that they were dead before cooking and they could harbor bacteria.
- Do not overcook seafood—it will become hard, rubbery, and lose much of its flavor. Remember that fish will continue to cook after it is removed from the heat, especially when surrounded by hot broth in a soup or stew. Food safety specialists recommend that fish be cooked until the flesh is opaque and flakes easily. It should have an internal temperature of 145 degrees.
- When a recipe calls for a firm white fish, choose from cod, scrod, monkfish, sea bass, halibut, orange roughy, haddock, or snapper.

Oriental Shrimp and Vegetable Pasta

⅓ cup peanut oil
¼ cup reduced-sodium soy sauce
¼ cup rice vinegar
2 tablespoons dark sesame oil
1 tablespoon sugar
1 tablespoon peeled and minced fresh ginger
½ to 1 teaspoon hot chili oil or red pepper flakes
2 cloves garlic, peeled
2½ cups sliced asparagus (1-inch-long pieces)
¾ pound medium shrimp, peeled and deveined
¾ pound angel hair pasta
½ cup fresh or frozen peas
½ cup seeded and thinly sliced red bell peppers (1-inch pieces)
½ cup coarsely chopped roasted salted peanuts or cashews
2 tablespoons thinly sliced scallions

This easy-to-put-together dinner features quickly blanched vegetables, shrimp, and angel hair pasta tossed in a light Asian dressing and topped with chopped peanuts. Most grocery stores now carry a wide variety of Asian spices and condiments, so cooking restaurant favorites at home has never been easier. Look for thin asparagus for extra-quick cooking. When cooking both vegetables and pasta in the same pot, it is helpful to have a pasta set with a removable insert. Otherwise, a strainer with a long handle will do.

Cooking Time: 30 minutes or less
Serves: 4

1. In the serving bowl, combine the peanut oil, soy sauce, rice vinegar, sesame oil, sugar, ginger, and chili oil. Set aside.
2. In a large pot over high heat, put the water up to boil for the pasta.
3. When the water is boiling, blanch the garlic for 30 to 45 seconds. (For easy blanching, skewer the garlic or use a mesh spoon to scoop it out). Rinse the garlic under cold water, pat dry, mince, and add to the serving bowl.
4. Add the asparagus and cook for 3 to 5 minutes, or until crisp-tender. Remove to the serving bowl.

5. Add the shrimp and cook for 1 to 2 minutes, or until just cooked through. Remove to the serving bowl. Stir to coat the shrimp and asparagus with the dressing.

6. Add the pasta and cook for 4 minutes. Add the peas and cook for 1 to 2 minutes, or until the pasta is al dente. Drain and add the pasta and peas to the serving bowl. Stir well to combine. Top with the red peppers, peanuts, and scallions.

•••••••••••••••••

Variations:

Oriental Vegetarian Pasta: *Substitute 4 cups of broccoli florets for the shrimp. In step 4, add the broccoli and cook for 2 minutes before adding the asparagus.*

Oriental Pasta with Tofu: *For added protein, add a 6-ounce package of tofu, drained and cut into cubes, to the dressing.*

•••••••••••••••••

Shrimp and Asparagus Risotto

4 cups clam juice mixed with
    1 cup of water, or 4 to
    5 cups reduced-sodium
    chicken broth
2 tablespoons butter
½ cup finely chopped onions
1½ cups Arborio rice
½ cup dry white wine
2 cups sliced asparagus
    (1-inch-long pieces)
¾ pound shrimp, peeled and
    deveined
¼ pound prosciutto, finely
    chopped
1 cup grated Parmesan cheese
½ teaspoon ground black
    pepper

Risotto, a slow-cooking creamy rice dish, is a main-stay of Northern Italian cooking. Its essence is Arborio rice, a short-grain, highly glutinous rice grown in the Po Valley of Northern Italy. What makes Arborio rice exceptional is its ability to absorb liquid while retaining its firmness. The secret to perfect risotto is the slow and steady sequential additions of broth. One note: It is not essential to warm the broth first, but it does help maintain a constant cooking temperature. Look for thin asparagus spears for more even cooking.

Cooking Time: 30 minutes or less
Serves: 4

1. In a microwave, bring the broth to a simmer.
2. In a large saucepan or stock pot over medium heat, add the butter. Add the onions and sauté until softened, 2 to 3 minutes, stirring frequently.
3. Add the rice. Stir constantly to coat with the butter, 1 minute.
4. Add the wine and stir until completely absorbed.
5. Add the asparagus, reserving the tips. Stir to combine.
6. Begin slowly adding the broth, ½ cup at a time, stirring frequently. Wait until each addition is almost completely absorbed before adding more, about 3 to 5 minutes for each addition.

7. After 15 minutes, add the reserved asparagus tips, shrimp, and prosciutto. Stir to combine and to prevent sticking. Continue to add broth, stirring frequently, for 5 to 8 minutes, or until the risotto has a creamy texture but is still al dente, slightly firm to the bite. You may not need to use all of the liquid.

8. Add the Parmesan cheese and pepper and stir vigorously to combine. Serve immediately.

· · · · · · · · · · · · · · · ·

Variation:

Chicken and Asparagus Risotto: *Substitute ½ pound of boneless and skinless chicken breasts, cut into 1-inch pieces, for the shrimp. In step 2, add the onions and chicken and sauté for 3 to 5 minutes, or until the chicken begins to cook through.*

· · · · · · · · · · · · · · · ·

Beer-Battered Fish Tacos

8 6-inch corn tortillas
1½ cups all-purpose flour
½ teaspoon salt
¼ teaspoon ground black
    pepper
1 to 1¼ cups beer
3 cups vegetable oil
1½ pounds cod, flounder, or
    other white fish fillets,
    cut crosswise into 1-
    inch-wide strips
¼ cup sour cream
¼ cup mayonnaise
1 cup fresh tomato salsa,
    ready-made or recipe,
    page 175
2 cups cabbage, shredded
1 cup guacamole (optional)
¼ pound cheddar cheese,
    grated or shredded
    (optional)
1 lime, cut into eighths

One of the best culinary rewards for moving to Southern California was the discovery of Mexico's Baja cuisine, especially fish tacos. Irresistible fried fish fillets, surrounded by crunchy shredded cabbage and drizzled with creamy white sauce and salsa, are enclosed in warm corn tortillas. The flavors and textures are in perfect symmetry. Once you try them, you'll be singing "California, here I come!"

Cooking Time: 30 minutes or less
Serves: 4

1. Preheat the oven to 350 degrees.
2. Wrap the tortillas in aluminum foil and place in the oven to warm for 10 minutes. (Tortillas can also be wrapped in a damp towel and warmed in the microwave on high for 15 to 30 seconds).
3. In a medium bowl, combine 1 cup of the flour, salt, and pepper. Gradually whisk in the beer to form a medium-thick, smooth batter. (Batter can also be mixed in a food processor or blender).
4. In a medium saucepan or skillet, heat the oil to 375 degrees. The oil should be at least 1 inch deep.
5. Dust the fish with the remaining ½ cup flour. Working in batches, dip the fish into the batter, coating each piece completely and allowing any excess batter to drip off.

6. Fry the fish, 2 to 3 pieces at a time, for 3 to 5 minutes, or until golden and crispy. Using tongs, turn the fish twice to ensure even cooking. Transfer the fish to paper towels and repeat with remaining pieces.

7. Meanwhile, combine the sour cream and mayonnaise. Spread 1 tablespoon of sour cream sauce on each tortilla. Top with 1 to 2 tablespoons of salsa, ¼ cup of cabbage, fish, 2 tablespoons of guacamole, 2 tablespoons of cheddar cheese, and a squeeze of lime; or to taste.

· · · · · · · · · · · · · · · ·

Variation:

Shrimp Tacos: *Substitute 1 pound of large shrimp, peeled and deveined, for the fish. Fry the shrimp for 2 to 4 minutes, or until golden and crispy.*

· · · · · · · · · · · · · · · ·

Seafood Stew

2 tablespoons olive oil
1 cup finely chopped onions
½ cup finely chopped carrots
½ cup finely chopped celery
1 tablespoon minced garlic
1 cup dry white wine
1 cup clam juice
1 28-ounce can diced
    tomatoes, drained
1 pound firm white fish, cut
    into 1-inch pieces
12 mussels, scrubbed and
    debearded
12 littleneck or small clams,
    scrubbed
12 shrimp, peeled and
    deveined
1 teaspoon salt
½ teaspoon ground black
    pepper
2 tablespoons chopped fresh
    Italian parsley
    (optional)

This fast and easy seafood stew features a variety of fish and shellfish served in a garlic–tomato broth. It is simple enough for a family dinner and elegant enough for guests. Choose whichever firm white fish looks good at the market: cod, sea bass, halibut, or orange roughy are all delicious. The secret to the success of all seafood stews is not to overcook the seafood, so use care when cooking.

Cooking Time: 30 minutes or less
Serves: 4

1. In a large stock pot over medium heat, add the oil. Sauté the onions, carrots, celery, and garlic until softened, 5 to 8 minutes, stirring frequently.
2. Add the wine, clam juice, and tomatoes and stir to combine. Bring to a boil.
3. Reduce the heat, cover, and simmer for 15 minutes, stirring occasionally.
4. Add the fish, mussels, and clams and cook for 3 to 5 minutes, or until the mussel and clam shells begin to open. Add the shrimp and cook for 1 to 2 minutes, or until the seafood is just cooked through.
5. Season with salt and pepper. Sprinkle with the parsley.

Coconut Fish and Shrimp Stew

This savory fish stew is a Brazilian specialty. White fish fillets are marinated in lime juice and hot peppers and simmered with vibrant vegetables in creamy coconut milk. This mild stew is traditionally made with cod, although haddock, orange roughy, or scrod are all pleasing.

Cooking Time: 30 minutes or less
Serves: 4

1. In a medium bowl, add the fish, lime juice, and jalapeños and stir to combine. Set aside.
2. In a large stock pot or large skillet over medium heat, add the oil. Sauté the onions, both bell peppers, and garlic until softened, 5 to 8 minutes, stirring frequently.
3. Add the clam juice, coconut milk, and rice. Cover and simmer for 10 minutes, stirring occasionally.
4. Add the fish and its marinade, tomatoes, and green beans. Cook uncovered for 5 minutes, stirring occasionally.
5. Add the shrimp and cook for 1 to 2 minutes, or until the seafood is just cooked through.
6. Season with salt and pepper. Sprinkle with cilantro.

1 pound cod, or other white fish, cut into 1-inch pieces
3 tablespoons freshly squeezed lime juice
1 tablespoon seeded and minced fresh jalapeño peppers
2 tablespoons olive oil
1 cup chopped onions
½ cup seeded and chopped green bell peppers
½ cup seeded and chopped red bell peppers
1 tablespoon minced garlic
2 cups clam juice
1 cup canned unsweetened coconut milk, stirred vigorously to blend
½ cup rice (preferably jasmine or basmati)
2 cups seeded and chopped ripe plum tomatoes
1 cup trimmed and sliced green beans (1-inch pieces)
1 pound shrimp, peeled and deveined
1 teaspoon salt
½ teaspoon ground black pepper
¼ cup chopped fresh cilantro (optional)

Spicy Shrimp with Dried-Fruit Pilaf

1 pound large shrimp, peeled
    and deveined
1 teaspoon paprika
1 teaspoon ground ginger
½ teaspoon ground cinnamon
¼ teaspoon cayenne pepper
2 tablespoons olive oil
1 tablespoon butter
1 cup finely chopped onions
1½ cups rice
3 cups reduced-sodium
    chicken broth
½ cup chopped dried apricots
½ cup currants or golden
    raisins
¼ cup dried cranberries
    (optional)
1 tablespoon orange zest
1 teaspoon salt
½ cup slivered almonds,
    lightly toasted

This Mediterranean entrée combines fragrantly seasoned shrimp with a fruity rice pilaf. A pilaf refers to rice that has been cooked in oil or butter, usually with seasonings or onions, before being simmered in liquid. The name originally came from the Persian pilau.

Cooking Time: 30 minutes or less
Serves: 4

1. In a medium bowl, combine the shrimp, paprika, ginger, cinnamon, and cayenne pepper.
2. In a large skillet over medium-high heat, add the oil. Add the shrimp and cook for 1 minute per side. Remove the shrimp and reserve.
3. Melt the butter in the skillet. Add the onions and sauté until softened, 3 to 5 minutes, stirring frequently.
4. Add the rice and stir to combine. Cook for 1 minute, stirring frequently.
5. Add the broth. Bring to a boil and stir to deglaze and dislodge any bits of food or seasonings that have stuck to the bottom of the skillet.
6. Add the apricots, currants, cranberries, orange zest, and salt and stir to combine.

7. Reduce the heat, cover, and simmer for 15 to 20 minutes, or until the rice is almost tender, stirring occasionally.
8. Add the shrimp and stir to combine. Cover and cook for 2 minutes. Top with the almonds.

· · · · · · · · · · · · · · · ·

Variation:

Chicken with Dried-Fruit Pilaf: *Substitute 1 to 1½ pounds of skinless and boneless chicken breasts for the shrimp and brown for 4 to 5 minutes per side. Remove the chicken, cover with foil, and reserve until step 8.*

· · · · · · · · · · · · · · · ·

Shrimp and Feta Cheese

3 tablespoons olive oil
1½ pounds large shrimp,
    peeled and deveined
1 cup finely chopped onions
2 teaspoons minced garlic
1 28-ounce can diced
    tomatoes, drained
½ cup dry white wine
1 tablespoon freshly squeezed
    lemon juice
1 teaspoon salt
½ teaspoon ground black
    pepper
⅛ teaspoon cayenne pepper
½ pound feta cheese,
    crumbled

Big tasty shrimp find their match in this Greek inspired union of feta cheese, garlic, and tomatoes cooked to bubbly perfection. Serve with warm pita bread and a cucumber, red onion, and kalamata olive salad tossed with red wine vinaigrette. It also is great with buttered rice.

Cooking Time: 30 minutes or less
Serves: 4

1. Preheat the oven to 400 degrees.
2. In a large ovenproof skillet over medium heat, add the oil. Sauté the shrimp for 15 to 30 seconds per side, or until they just turn pink. Remove the shrimp and reserve.
3. Add the onions and cook until softened, 3 to 5 minutes.
4. Add the garlic and cook for 1 minute, stirring constantly.
5. Add the tomatoes, wine, lemon juice, salt, black pepper, and cayenne pepper and stir to combine. Bring to a boil.
6. Cook for 5 to 8 minutes, or until thickened, stirring frequently.

7. Arrange the shrimp on top of the tomato sauce. Cover with the feta cheese.

8. Bake for 10 to 15 minutes, or until the tomatoes are bubbly, the shrimp is cooked through, and the feta has melted. For added browning, place under the broiler for 1 to 2 minutes.

Thai Shrimp and Jasmine Rice

2 tablespoons vegetable oil
1 pound large shrimp, peeled
    and deveined
2 tablespoons seeded and
    finely chopped fresh
    jalapeño peppers
1 tablespoon minced garlic
1 tablespoon peeled and
    minced fresh ginger
1½ cups jasmine or basmati
    rice, rinsed and
    drained
1½ cups clam juice
1 cup unsweetened coconut
    milk, stirred vigorously
    to combine
2 tablespoons freshly
    squeezed lemon juice
1 teaspoon lemon zest
1 cup seeded and chopped
    ripe plum tomatoes
½ cup thinly sliced scallions
½ cup chopped roasted salted
    peanuts
2 tablespoons freshly
    squeezed lime juice
1 teaspoon salt
¼ cup coarsely chopped fresh
    basil (optional)

This Far East risotto-like dish combines the aromatic and evocative flavorings of Thai cooking in the spirit of sanuk, a joyous sense of well-being. Fusing the best from many Asian cultures, Thai cuisine finds harmony between delicate and assertive flavors. Jasmine rice, a fragrant long-grain white rice indigenous to Thailand, cooks quickly and requires less liquid than its fluffier and better-known American cousin, converted rice.

Cooking Time: 30 minutes or less
Serves: 4

1. In a large skillet over medium-high heat, add the oil. Sauté the shrimp, jalapeños, garlic, and ginger for 2 minutes, stirring frequently. Remove the shrimp and reserve.
2. Add the rice and cook for 1 minute, stirring constantly. Add the clam juice, coconut milk, and lemon juice and stir to combine. Bring to a boil.
3. Reduce the heat, cover, and simmer for 12 to 15 minutes, stirring occasionally.
4. Add the shrimp, lemon zest, and tomatoes and stir to combine. Cook for 5 minutes, or until the rice is tender, the broth has been absorbed, and the shrimp is cooked through.
5. Remove from the heat. Add the scallions, peanuts, lime juice, and salt and stir to combine. Sprinkle with the basil.

Shrimp and White Bean Stew

This quick-cooking Tuscan-style stew is an extraordinary medley of tastes, textures, and colors. Succulent sautéed shrimp are married with salty and mellow pancetta, tomatoes, beans, and basil. While the flavors fuse, each ingredient maintains its own identity.

3 tablespoons olive oil
¼ pound pancetta, chopped (optional)
1½ pounds shrimp, peeled and deveined
3 cups rinsed and drained canned cannellini beans
1 cup seeded and chopped ripe plum tomatoes, or 1 cup drained canned diced tomatoes
½ cup clam juice
2 tablespoons coarsely chopped fresh basil
2 teaspoons minced garlic
1 teaspoon salt
½ teaspoon ground black pepper

Cooking Time: 30 minutes or less
Serves: 4

1. In a large skillet over medium heat, add the oil. Sauté the pancetta for 8 to 10 minutes, or until lightly browned, stirring frequently.
2. Add the shrimp and cook for 30 seconds per side.
3. Add the beans, tomatoes, clam juice, basil, garlic, salt, and pepper. Cook until heated through, 5 to 8 minutes.

....

Variation:

Meatless Shrimp and White Bean Stew: *For non-meat eaters, omit the pancetta.*

....

Thai Shrimp and Cellophane Noodles

¼ pound dried cellophane
    noodles
3 tablespoons vegetable oil
1 pound large shrimp, peeled
    and deveined
3 cups cubed Japanese
    eggplant
2 cups trimmed and sliced
    green beans (1-inch-
    long pieces)
1 tablespoon seeded and finely
    chopped fresh jalapeño
    peppers (optional)
1 14½-ounce can plus 1 cup
    unsweetened coconut
    milk, stirred vigorously
    to blend
1 to 2 tablespoons Thai red
    curry paste
1 teaspoon salt
1 cup fresh or frozen peas
2 tablespoons thinly sliced
    scallions
2 tablespoons coarsely
    chopped fresh basil
    (optional)

In this creamy dish, juicy shrimp, cellophane noodles, and vegetables are simmered in a spicy curry–coconut sauce. Cellophane noodles—also known as mung bean noodles, bean threads, saifun, or glass noodles—are sold dried in tightly looped skeins and then soaked in hot water to soften. These versatile noodles are only one of the many varieties used in Thai cooking. Luckily, with supermarkets offering a wide range of international foods, these clear thin noodles, curry paste, and coconut milk are easier to find than ever before.

Cooking Time: 30 minutes or less
Serves: 4

1. In a medium bowl, place the noodles and add enough hot water to cover. Let stand until the noodles are pliable, 10 to 15 minutes. Drain, rinse with cold water, and drain again. Set aside.
2. Meanwhile, in a large skillet over medium-high heat, add the oil. Add the shrimp and cook for 1 minute per side. Remove the shrimp and reserve.
3. Add the eggplant, green beans, and jalapeños and cook until softened, 5 to 8 minutes, stirring frequently.

4. Add the coconut milk, curry paste to taste (2 table-spoons is *hot!*), and salt and stir to combine. Reduce the heat and simmer for 15 minutes, or until the vegetables are tender and the sauce thickens slightly, stirring occasionally.
5. Add the reserved shrimp, noodles, and peas. Cook for 2 to 5 minutes, or until the shrimp and vegetables are cooked through, stirring frequently.
6. Sprinkle with the scallions and basil.

Oven-Baked Fish
with Roasted Vegetables

6 ripe plum tomatoes, sliced ¼-inch thick (about 1 pound)
2 cups cleaned and thinly sliced leeks (white part only)
2 cups thickly sliced zucchini
2 cups thinly sliced new potatoes
1 cup seeded and thinly sliced bell peppers (red, orange, or yellow)
2 cups thinly sliced shiitake or other mushrooms
2 teaspoons minced garlic
3 tablespoons olive oil
1 teaspoon dried thyme
2 tablespoons freshly squeezed lemon juice
2 tablespoons coarsely chopped fresh basil (optional)
1 teaspoon lemon zest
1 teaspoon balsamic vinegar (optional)
1 tablespoon salt
4 6-ounce skinless fish fillets (salmon, sea bass, cod, or flounder)
½ teaspoon ground black pepper
½ cup toasted bread crumbs, homemade or packaged

Roasting vegetables at high temperatures caramelizes their natural sugars and brings out their inherent sweetness. This dish highlights its flavorful vegetables and is balanced by the addition of simply seasoned fish fillets. Look for fillets of uniform thickness to ensure even cooking, or bake fish for varying lengths of time to prevent overcooking thinner fillets.

Cooking Time: 60 minutes or less
Serves: 4

1. Preheat the oven to 450 degrees.
2. In a 13 × 9 × 2-inch baking pan, combine the tomatoes, leeks, zucchini, potatoes, bell peppers, mushrooms, and garlic. Drizzle with 2 tablespoons of the oil and toss to combine. Sprinkle with the thyme.
3. Roast the vegetables for 25 to 30 minutes, or until they begin to soften and brown. Add the lemon juice, basil, lemon zest, vinegar, and 1 teaspoon of the salt and toss to combine.
4. Lightly coat the fish with the remaining 1 tablespoon oil and sprinkle with the remaining 2 teaspoons salt, pepper, and bread crumbs.
5. Arrange the fish over the vegetables and roast for 10 to 15 minutes, or until the fish is cooked through.

Bouillabaisse

The signature ingredients of this famous Provençal fish stew are monkfish, a firm white fish; fennel, a licorice-flavored bulb; and saffron, a distinctive spice from Spain. Harvesting saffron's delicate threads is so labor intensive it is regarded as the world's most expensive seasoning. Luckily, this fabulous stew only requires a small amount. Serve this with bruschetta rubbed with garlic and drizzled with olive oil.

Cooking Time: 60 minutes or less
Serves: 4

1. In a large stock pot over medium heat, add the oil. Sauté the leeks, fennel, onions, and garlic until softened, 7 to 10 minutes, stirring frequently.
2. Add the tomatoes and their juice, thyme, fennel seeds, bay leaf, and orange peel and stir to combine. Simmer for 5 minutes.
3. Add the clam juice and saffron and stir to combine. Bring to a boil.
4. Reduce the heat, cover, and simmer for 20 minutes, stirring occasionally.
5. Add the monkfish and clams and cook for 3 to 5 minutes, or until the clam shells begin to open. Add the shrimp and cook for 1 to 2 minutes, or until the seafood is just cooked through.
6. Sprinkle with the parsley.

¼ cup olive oil
2 cups cleaned and thinly sliced leeks (white part only)
2 cups coarsely chopped fresh fennel
1 cup finely chopped onions
1 tablespoon minced garlic
1 28-ounce can diced tomatoes
1 teaspoon dried thyme
½ teaspoon dried fennel seeds
1 bay leaf
1 3-inch strip orange peel (optional)
3 cups clam juice
¼ teaspoon saffron
1 pound monkfish, or other firm white fish, cut into 1-inch pieces
2 pounds littleneck or small clams, scrubbed
1 pound shrimp, peeled and deveined
2 tablespoons finely chopped fresh Italian parsley (optional)

Shrimp and Sausage Gumbo

3 tablespoons vegetable oil
3 tablespoons all-purpose flour
2 cups finely chopped onions
1 cup seeded and finely
    chopped green bell
    peppers
½ cup finely chopped celery
1 teaspoon minced garlic
2 cups clam juice
1 14½-ounce can diced
    tomatoes, drained
½ pound smoked andouille
    sausage, smoked
    Louisiana sausage, or
    kielbasa, halved
    lengthwise and sliced
    ¼-inch thick
½ teaspoon cayenne pepper
1 bay leaf
1 cup thickly sliced okra
1 pound shrimp, peeled and
    deveined

Few things mean New Orleans like beignets, po' boys, and Louisiana's trademark gumbo. The secret to gumbo's distinctive flavor is the roux, a mahogany-colored, slow-cooked mixture of flour and oil that is found in many Cajun dishes. Cajuns, descendants of French Acadians who settled in central Louisiana's bayou country after being forced out of Nova Scotia in 1785, became major influences in the area's cooking style. This gumbo, loaded with shrimp, andouille sausage, and okra, is a hearty soup on its own or more of a stew if rice is added. Make sure to have all your vegetables prepped and ready to go. Serve Tabasco on the side for those who like it hot!

Cooking Time: 60 minutes or less
Serves: 4

1. In a large soup pot, over high heat, add the oil. When the oil is very hot, almost smoking, add the flour and stir constantly until the mixture turns a deep reddish-brown, 2 to 5 minutes. You will smell the flour cooking, and it may smell as if something is almost burning, but don't be alarmed.

2. Reduce the heat to medium-high and immediately add the onions, green peppers, celery, and garlic. Cook until softened, 5 to 8 minutes, stirring constantly.

3. Add the clam juice, tomatoes, sausage, cayenne pepper, and bay leaf and stir to combine. Bring to a boil.
4. Reduce the heat, cover, and simmer for 10 minutes, stirring occasionally.
5. Add the okra and simmer uncovered for 10 minutes, stirring occasionally.
6. Add the shrimp and simmer for 1 to 2 minutes, or until just cooked through.

. . . .

Variation:

Shrimp, Sausage, and Rice Gumbo: *Add ½ cup of rice in step 4.*

. . . .

Paella

1 tablespoon olive oil
½ pound hot or sweet Italian sausage, sliced ½ inch thick
4 chicken legs or thighs
1 cup chopped onions
1 cup seeded and chopped green bell peppers
2 teaspoons minced garlic
⅛ teaspoon red pepper flakes
1½ cups rice
2½ cups reduced-sodium chicken broth
1 cup canned diced tomatoes
½ teaspoon saffron (optional)
1 bay leaf
12 littleneck or small clams, scrubbed
12 mussels, scrubbed and debearded
12 shrimp, peeled and deveined
1 teaspoon salt
½ teaspoon ground black pepper

Paella, the signature dish of the Valencia region of Spain, is named for the broad, shallow pan in which it is traditionally cooked. It began as a peasant dish, made primarily of rice, vegetables, and with luck, a few scraps of fish. Now paella is made with a wide variety of seafood, in addition to chicken, sausage, and pork. This version uses clams, mussels, and shrimp, but you can choose your favorite seafood to complete this dish—or if you'd rather, you can leave the seafood out entirely.

Cooking Time: 60 minutes or less
Serves: 4

1. In a large skillet over medium-high heat, add the oil. Add the sausage and cook, 5 to 8 minutes, turning often.
2. Add the chicken and brown, 3 to 5 minutes per side. Continue cooking for 5 minutes, turning the chicken and sausage frequently. Push the meat to the side.
3. Reduce the heat to medium and add the onions, green peppers, garlic, and red pepper flakes. Cook until softened, 5 to 8 minutes, stirring frequently.

4. Add the rice and stir to combine.
5. Add the broth, tomatoes and their juice, saffron, and bay leaf and stir to combine.
6. Cover and simmer for 20 minutes.
7. Add the clams and mussels, stir to combine, cover, and cook for 3 to 5 minutes, or until the clam and mussel shells begin to open. Add the shrimp and cook for 1 to 2 minutes, or until the shellfish is just cooked through.
8. Season with salt and pepper.

Manhattan Clam Chowder

¼ pound bacon or salt pork,
    chopped
2 cups peeled, cubed potatoes
1 cup finely chopped onions
1 cup finely chopped celery
1 teaspoon dried basil
½ teaspoon dried thyme
2 cups clam juice
1 28-ounce can diced
    tomatoes
2 6¼-ounce cans minced
    clams
1 teaspoon salt
½ teaspoon ground black
    pepper

The battle of chowders between New England's creamy white and the Big Apple's red is ongoing. Manhattan's version is less sinful, substituting tomatoes for heavy cream, but is equally delicious. Like its nemesis, it is even better if you use fresh clams.

Cooking Time: 60 minutes or less
Serves: 4

1. In a large stock pot over medium-low heat, sauté the bacon until brown and crisp, 8 to 10 minutes, stirring frequently. Try not to scorch the bottom of the pot.
2. Discard all but 1 tablespoon of fat. Add the potatoes, onions, celery, basil, and thyme and sauté until softened, 5 to 8 minutes, stirring frequently.
3. Add the clam juice, tomatoes and their juice, and juice from the clams (reserving the clams), and stir to combine. Bring to a boil.
4. Reduce the heat, partially cover, and simmer for 15 to 20 minutes, or until the potatoes are tender, stirring occasionally.
5. Add the reserved clams. Cook over very low heat until heated through, 1 to 2 minutes. Do not boil. Season with salt and pepper.

•••••••••••••••••

Variation:

Manhattan Clam Chowder with Fresh Clams: *Substitute 24 fresh clams for the canned clams. Just steam them in 1 cup of water until they open, reserve the broth, and chop the clams. Proceed with the directions, substituting the broth for clam juice, and adding the cooked clams just before serving. For a more rustic presentation, leave some or all of the clams in their shells for guests to remove.*

•••••••••••••••••

New England Clam and Fish Chowder

¼ pound bacon or salt pork, chopped
2 cups peeled, cubed potatoes
½ cup finely chopped onions
¼ cup finely chopped celery
½ teaspoon dried thyme
1 tablespoon all-purpose flour
1 cup clam juice
2 6¼-ounce cans minced clams
1 pound cod, or other firm white fish, cut into 1-inch pieces
1 cup heavy cream
1 cup milk, or half and half, or heavy cream
1 teaspoon salt
½ teaspoon white or black pepper

Creamy and rich, studded with clams, fish, and potato chunks, New England clam chowder is as integral a part of the Northeast as Boston accents, the Celtics, and summertime clambakes on the beach. It's even better if you use fresh clams or quahogs.

Cooking Time: 60 minutes or less
Serves: 4

1. In a large stock pot over medium-low heat, sauté the bacon until brown and crisp, 8 to 10 minutes, stirring frequently. Try not to scorch the bottom of the pot.
2. Discard all but 1 tablespoon of fat. Add the potatoes, onions, celery, and thyme and sauté until softened, 5 to 8 minutes, stirring frequently.
3. Sprinkle with the flour and stir to combine.
4. Add the clam juice and juice from the clams (reserving the clams) and stir to combine. Bring to a boil.
5. Reduce the heat, partially cover, and simmer for 10 to 15 minutes, or until the potatoes are just tender, stirring occasionally.
6. Add the cod and simmer for 5 to 8 minutes, or until the fish and potatoes are cooked through.
7. Add the cream, milk, and reserved clams. Cook over very low heat until heated through, 1 to 2 minutes. Do not boil. Season with salt and pepper.

....

Variation:

New England Clam Chowder with Fresh Clams: *Substitute 24 fresh clams for the canned clams. Steam the clams in 1 cup of water or wine until they open, reserve the broth, and chop the clams. Proceed with the directions, substituting the broth for clam juice, and adding the cooked clams just before serving. For a more rustic presentation, leave some or all of the clams in their shells for guests to remove.*

....

Smoked Salmon and Goat Cheese Quiche

Crust:

1¼ cups all-purpose flour
¼ teaspoon salt
½ cup (1 stick) unsalted
    butter, chilled and cut
    into ½-inch pieces
2 to 4 tablespoons ice water

Filling:

4 eggs
1 cup cream or milk
1 cup milk
½ teaspoon salt
¼ teaspoon ground black
    pepper
1 tablespoon finely chopped
    fresh dill
3 tablespoons finely chopped
    fresh chives
¼ pound goat cheese,
    crumbled
¼ pound smoked salmon,
    coarsely chopped

Quiche, a custard filling nestled in a pastry crust, hails from the Alsace and Lorraine regions of France. This elegant quiche updates the classic French rendering with today's most popular ingredients. In this version, lightly salted smoked salmon is the perfect foil for creamy goat cheese and piquant dill and chives. Make your own crust or buy a ready-made crust and fit it into a 9-inch pie plate.

Cooking Time: 60 minutes or less
Serves: 4

1. Prepare the crust: In a food processor fitted with a metal chopping blade, mix the flour and salt (5 seconds). Add the butter and pulse until the mixture resembles coarse meal (10 short pulses). Sprinkle the minimum amount of water over the mixture and pulse until distributed throughout the dough and the crumbs start sticking together (5 to 10 pulses). Process just until the dough holds together, adding the remaining water if necessary. Do not allow the dough to form a ball.

2. Scrape the dough onto the work surface. Shape the dough into a 1-inch-thick disc. Wrap the dough tightly with plastic wrap and refrigerate for 30 minutes, or until it is firm enough to roll out.

Seafood

3. Preheat the oven to 450 degrees.
4. Roll out the dough and fit into a 9-inch pie pan. Prick the dough with a fork and bake for 5 to 10 minutes, or until lightly browned. Remove from the oven and reduce the temperature to 350 degrees.
5. Prepare the filling: Meanwhile, in a medium bowl, beat the eggs, cream, milk, salt, and pepper. Add the dill and chives and stir to combine. Set aside.
6. Line the partially baked pie crust with the cheese. Top with the smoked salmon. Add the eggs.
7. Bake for 40 to 50 minutes, or until the eggs are set and the center doesn't jiggle. If the crust begins to brown before the quiche is ready, cover it with aluminum foil to prevent burning. Let stand 5 to 10 minutes before serving.

Cioppino

3 tablespoons olive oil
2 cups finely chopped onions
1 cup seeded and finely
    chopped green bell
    peppers
1 cup seeded and finely
    chopped red bell
    peppers
1 tablespoon minced garlic
1 cup dry red wine
1 cup clam juice
1 28-ounce can diced
    tomatoes
3 tablespoons tomato paste
1 teaspoon dried oregano
1 teaspoon dried basil
1 pound firm white fish, cut
    into 1-inch pieces
3 pounds cleaned mixed
    shellfish (mussels,
    shrimp, clams, crab
    claws, scallops, cut-up
    lobster)
1 teaspoon salt
½ teaspoon ground black
    pepper
¼ cup chopped fresh Italian
    parsley or fresh basil

Cioppino, a fisherman's stew that hails from San Francisco, is our nation's version of France's classic bouillabaisse. Plan to get your fingers messy—this richly flavored stew is loaded with shellfish. Choose from crab legs, scallops, clams, mussels, shrimp, or lobster, and whichever white fish is your favorite. If you like a little spice, add a few shakes of cayenne pepper.

Cooking Time: 60 minutes or less
Serves: 4

1. In a large stock pot over medium heat, add the oil. Sauté the onions, both bell peppers, and garlic until softened, 7 to 10 minutes, stirring frequently.
2. Add the wine, clam juice, tomatoes and their juice, tomato paste, oregano, and basil and stir to combine. Bring to a boil.
3. Reduce the heat, cover, and simmer for 30 minutes, stirring occasionally.
4. Add the fish and shellfish and cook for 5 to 7 minutes, or until the fish is cooked through and clam and/or mussel shells have opened. (If using shrimp or scallops, add during the last 1 to 2 minutes of cooking).
5. Season with the salt and pepper. Sprinkle with the parsley or basil.

5

VEGETARIAN

30 Minutes or Less:

Gazpacho

Cucumber and Yogurt
 Soup

Minestrone Soup

Mexican Tortilla Lasagna

Vegetarian Couscous

Vegetable Frittata

Pasta with Pesto

Pasta with Tomatoes,
 Basil, and Garlic

Pasta with Broccoli, Garlic,
 and Toasted Walnuts

Cheese Pizza

Bean and Cheese Enchi-
 ladas in Green Sauce

Tomato and Basil Frittata

60 Minutes or Less:

Lentil-Vegetable Soup

Butternut Squash and
 Apple Soup

Ratatouille

Black Bean and Butternut
 Squash Chili

Eggplant and Vegetable
 Tian

Chile Relleno Phyllo Bake

Spinach and Ricotta
 Lasagna

Tomato, Goat Cheese, and
 Pesto Tart

The bounty of the garden has never been so grand. Not only is there increased variety, but there is greater recognition and appreciation of flavor. Vine-ripened tomatoes fill our supermarket bins, nudging out the plastic hothouse variety from years past. Where bland iceberg used to rule the lettuce roost, now dozens of tasty greens compete for shelf space. The white button mushroom need no longer feel lonely—his companions, the shiitake, portobello, oyster, and porcini are all tucked in nearby. This remarkable transformation was brought about by professional chefs (most notably Alice Waters of Chez Panisse in Berkeley, California) who designed their meals by what was fresh at the market that day and encouraged local farmers to grow organic vegetables with improved taste. With the advent of "designer" and organic produce and a new focus on cooking with vegetables, we are actually tasting vegetables as they were meant to be prepared: fresh and robust instead of overcooked and lifeless.

Vegetarian Tips:

- The United States government has revised the Food Guide Pyramid based on the latest nutritional research. This pyramid, which displays the relative importance of various food groups to the overall diet, deems the most significant component of a healthful diet to be grain products—bread, cereal, rice, and pasta—followed by vegetables and fruit. This shows the value of vegetarian entrées as part of a sensible overall eating pattern. Strict vegetarian diets can be healthy for adults and children if the proper balance of protein, calories, fat, and essential nutrients, especially B_{12}, are met.
- Beans and grains are an inexpensive and filling source of cholesterol-free protein. Low in fat, calories, and sodium, yet high in soluble and insoluble fiber, beans and grains are

great sources of complex carbohydrates and provide many valuable nutrients to vegetarian entrées.

- Eggs are a good source of protein, iron, zinc, and vitamins A, B, and D and have only 75 calories. Egg consumption dropped dramatically in response to the American Heart Association's concern that dietary cholesterol affects total cholesterol. But recent scientific research rebuts that premise and indicates that the consumption of saturated fat, not dietary cholesterol, influences the level of cholesterol in the blood. One large egg contains only 5 grams of total fat, of which only 1.5 grams are saturated.

- Support your local growers. Search out farmers' markets in your area and use ingredients in the heart of their growing season. In the spring and summer, find recipes that make use of the plethora of fresh tomatoes, basil, and summer squashes. In the fall and winter, look for dishes that use hearty eggplants, potatoes, broccoli, and winter squashes.

- Try organic vegetables for freshness and flavor, unless their cost is prohibitive.

- Choose crisp, unblemished vegetables that feel heavy, a sign that they are succulent and in their prime.

- Store most fresh vegetables in a cold, moist environment, either in their plastic bags or in a refrigerator crisper, and use them as soon as possible. Store onions, garlic, and potatoes in a cool cupboard. Once they are cut, place in the refrigerator. Do not refrigerate tomatoes, or their taste and texture will diminish.

- Always rinse vegetables thoroughly before using. Many vegetables are sprayed with pesticides and are picked under unsanitary conditions. If vegetables have been waxed, wash them with a mild detergent and rinse thoroughly before using. It is not necessary to peel carrots or potatoes after washing. Their skins contain important nutrients that are lost when pared. Use your own preference and time constraints when preparing these vegetables. Mushrooms, which tend to absorb a lot of water, should be quickly rinsed and dried or wiped with a damp cloth.

- If you use a food processor to chop vegetables with a high water content, like onions or bell peppers, pulse a small portion at a time to avoid turning them to pulp. Use the slicing blades to quickly cut carrots and mushrooms.

Gazpacho

Served cold, this Spanish soup, loaded with chunky fresh vegetables, is just the thing for hot summer evenings. Be sure to allow at least two hours for the soup to chill and for the flavors to come together. For an impressive presentation, garnish the soup with seasoned croutons; chopped yellow tomatoes, yellow peppers, or cucumbers; thinly sliced scallions; or poached shrimp.

Cooking Time: None
Serves: 4

1 large clove garlic
1 small red onion, peeled and quartered (about ¼ pound)
1 large green bell pepper, seeded and quartered (about ½ pound)
1 large red bell pepper, seeded and quartered (about ½ pound)
1 large cucumber, peeled, seeded, and quartered (about 1 pound)
1 28-ounce can Italian plum tomatoes
2 tablespoons olive oil
2 tablespoons red wine vinegar
2 teaspoons salt
½ teaspoon ground black pepper
½ teaspoon sugar
¼ teaspoon Tabasco or other hot red pepper sauce
2 cups tomato juice

1. In a food processor fitted with a metal chopping blade, with the motor running, purée the garlic. Add the onion and pulse until coarsely chopped. Add both bell peppers and cucumber and pulse until coarsely chopped.
2. Add the tomatoes and their juice, oil, vinegar, salt, pepper, sugar, and Tabasco. Pulse for 30 seconds, or until all of the vegetables are chopped but still chunky. Do not overprocess. (If this is too much bulk for your food processor, you may need to do this in two or more batches).
3. Transfer the soup to a large bowl. Add the tomato juice and stir to combine.
4. Cover and refrigerate for at least 2 hours.

Cucumber and Yogurt Soup

1 large clove garlic
⅛ cup chopped fresh dill
4 cups peeled, seeded, and
    coarsely chopped
    cucumbers
2 cups unflavored yogurt
2 cups water
1 tablespoon olive oil
1 tablespoon honey
2 teaspoons salt
1 teaspoon ground black
    pepper

This cold soup is perfect on a sweltering summer's day, when the mere thought of heating up your kitchen makes you sweat. It is quickly prepared in a food processor, so you can make it in the morning before heading out, stick it in the refrigerator, and have it ready on your return. Served with crusty French bread and a big crunchy salad topped with goat cheese, it's the perfect way to chill out after a long steamy day. Try topping it with chopped walnuts, chives, mint, or added dill.

Cooking Time: None
Serves: 4

1. In a food processor fitted with a metal blade, with the motor running, purée the garlic and dill.
2. Add the cucumbers and pulse until finely chopped.
3. Add the yogurt, water, oil, honey, salt, and pepper. Pulse until combined. Transfer to a large bowl, cover, and refrigerate for at least 2 hours. If the soup thickens too much, dilute with ice cubes.

Vegetarian

Minestrone Soup

Make minestrone soup a staple in summer when gardens are overflowing with zucchini, spinach, and beans. You can let your imagination run wild when preparing the soup—add whatever is plentiful to make it your own!

Cooking Time: 30 minutes or less
Serves: 4

2 tablespoons olive oil
4 cups cleaned and thinly sliced leeks (white part only)
1 cup thickly sliced carrots
1 cup thickly sliced celery
1 cup thickly sliced zucchini
6 cups vegetable broth or reduced-sodium chicken broth
1 28-ounce can diced tomatoes
1 tablespoon dried oregano
1 tablespoon dried basil
1 teaspoon salt
½ teaspoon ground black pepper
½ cup small pasta shapes or orzo
1 cup trimmed and sliced green beans (1-inch pieces)
1 cup spinach leaves
½ cup fresh or frozen peas
½ cup rinsed and drained canned chickpeas
⅓ cup grated Parmesan cheese

1. In a large stock pot over medium heat, add the oil. Sauté the leeks until softened, 3 to 5 minutes, stirring frequently.
2. Add the carrots, celery, and zucchini and cook until softened, 5 to 8 minutes, stirring occasionally.
3. Add the broth, tomatoes and their juice, oregano, basil, salt, and pepper and stir to combine.
4. Bring to a boil and cook for 5 minutes.
5. Add the pasta and green beans and cook for 5 minutes, stirring occasionally.
6. Reduce the heat, add the spinach, peas, and chickpeas and simmer for 5 minutes, stirring occasionally.
7. Top each serving with some of the Parmesan cheese.

Mexican Tortilla Lasagna

2 14½-ounce cans Mexican-
    style stewed tomatoes
1⅓ cups chopped fresh
    cilantro (optional)
1 4-ounce can diced green
    chiles, drained
15 6-inch corn tortillas
1 15¼-ounce can black beans,
    rinsed and drained, or
    refried pinto beans
1½ pounds Monterey Jack or
    cheddar cheese, grated
    or shredded
1½ cups sour cream
1 3¾-ounce can sliced and
    pitted black olives,
    drained

Like its Italian counterpart, this Mexican-inspired casserole layers tomato sauce and cheese. But instead of noodles, it uses corn tortillas as its base. This casserole is a bit spicy, so cut back on the chiles if you're cooking for sensitive palates. A bit of history: The recommended cheese, Monterey Jack, was developed in 1882 by David Jacks, a dairy farmer in Monterey, California, using an old recipe from the early mission days of the late 1700s.

Cooking Time: 30 minutes or less
Serves: 4 to 6

1. Preheat the oven to 375 degrees.
2. In a food processor fitted with a metal chopping blade, pulse the tomatoes, cilantro, and chiles to combine.
3. In a 13 × 9 × 2-inch baking pan, spread ½ cup of the tomato sauce over the bottom of the dish. Cover with 5 tortillas. You will need to cut 1 tortilla in half to cover the bottom completely.
4. Top with half of the beans, 2 cups of cheese, and 1½ cups of tomato sauce.
5. Cover the sauce with 5 tortillas. Top with the remaining beans, 2 cups of cheese, and 1½ cups of tomato sauce.
6. Cover the sauce with the remaining tortillas. Top with the remaining sauce and cheese.

Vegetarian

7. Cover with aluminum foil and bake for 15 minutes. Uncover and bake for 10 to 15 minutes, or until the cheese has melted and the casserole has heated through.
8. Remove from the oven. Cover with the sour cream and sprinkle with the olives. Let stand for 2 minutes before serving.

Vegetarian Couscous

Vegetables:

2 tablespoons olive oil
1 cup coarsely chopped red
    onions
1 teaspoon minced garlic
1 cup chopped turnips
    (optional)
1 cup thinly sliced carrots
1 cup seeded and coarsely
    chopped red bell
    peppers
1 cup drained canned diced
    tomatoes
1 teaspoon salt
½ teaspoon ground cumin
½ teaspoon curry powder
¼ teaspoon red pepper flakes
¼ teaspoon ground allspice
    (optional)
¼ teaspoon ground cinnamon
1½ cups vegetable broth or
    reduced-sodium
    chicken broth
2 cups thinly sliced zucchini
1 cup trimmed and sliced
    green beans (1-inch
    pieces)
4 cups spinach leaves
    (optional)
½ cup rinsed and drained
    canned chickpeas

(ingredients continue)

Couscous, long associated with Moroccan and Middle-Eastern dining, is believed by many to be a rice-like grain. This misconception is due primarily to its preparation and appearance—like rice, once it is combined with a liquid, it becomes a filling and fluffy side dish. But couscous is actually a form of pasta, made with semolina flour and water.

Cooking Time: 30 minutes or less
Serves: 4

1. Prepare the vegetables: In a large skillet over medium heat, add the oil. Add the onions and garlic and cook until softened, 3 to 5 minutes, stirring frequently.
2. Add the turnips, carrots, red peppers, tomatoes, salt, cumin, curry powder, red pepper flakes, allspice, cinnamon, and broth and stir to combine. Bring to a boil.
3. Reduce the heat, cover, and simmer for 10 minutes, stirring occasionally.
4. Add the zucchini, green beans, spinach, and chickpeas and cook for 5 to 10 minutes, or until the vegetables are crisp-tender, stirring occasionally.

5. Meanwhile, prepare the couscous: In a microwave, bring the broth to a boil. Add the butter and stir to combine. Combine the couscous, salt, and pepper in the serving bowl, pour the broth on top, and cover with aluminum foil for 5 to 10 minutes.

6. Fluff the couscous, top with the vegetables and their juice, and sprinkle with the almonds.

Couscous:

1½ cups vegetable broth or reduced-sodium chicken broth

2 tablespoons butter

1½ cups couscous

1 teaspoon salt

½ teaspoon ground black pepper

¼ cup almond slivers, lightly toasted

Vegetable Frittata

1 tablespoon olive oil
1 cup grated, shredded, or
    finely chopped new
    potatoes
½ cup thinly sliced
    mushrooms
½ cup coarsely chopped
    zucchini
¼ cup finely chopped red
    onions
¼ cup seeded and finely
    chopped red bell
    peppers
1 cup coarsely chopped
    spinach leaves
8 eggs
2 ounces Asiago, Fontina, or
    other hard cheese,
    grated or shredded
1 teaspoon salt
½ teaspoon dried thyme
¼ teaspoon ground black
    pepper

Frittatas are the Italian equivalent of France's ethereal omelets. But some major differences make frittatas a lot more attractive for cooks. A frittata is cooked first on the stove and then finished in the oven, eliminating any flipping gymnastics. This process results in an egg delight that is just firm and set, unlike an omelet, which is slightly moist and runny. I highly recommend using a nonstick pan, which allows you to move the frittata easily during cooking.

Cooking Time: 30 minutes or less
Serves: 4

1. Preheat the oven to 350 degrees.
2. In a 10- or 11-inch nonstick, ovenproof skillet over high heat, add the oil. Sauté the potatoes for 5 minutes, stirring frequently.
3. Reduce the heat to medium-high and add the mushrooms, zucchini, onions, and red peppers. Cook until softened, 5 to 8 minutes, stirring occasionally.
4. Add the spinach and cook for 2 minutes, or until wilted.

5. Meanwhile, in a medium bowl, beat the eggs. Add the cheese, salt, thyme, and pepper.
6. Reduce the heat to medium. Pour the eggs on top of the vegetables. Cook without stirring for 1 minute, or until the eggs are almost set on the bottom. Continue cooking, using a spatula to lift the edges of the frittata toward the center of the skillet, while gently tilting the pan so the uncooked eggs run underneath the bottom of the frittata. Cook for 30 to 40 seconds and repeat the process several times until the egg on top is still wet, but not runny.
7. Place in the oven. Bake for 3 to 7 minutes, or until the top is just set. Do not overcook.
8. Remove from the oven, run a spatula around the skillet edge to loosen the frittata, and slide or invert it onto a serving plate.

Pasta with Pesto

3 cloves garlic, peeled
¾ pound linguine or other
    pasta
2 cups packed fresh basil
¼ cup pine nuts or walnuts,
    lightly toasted
½ cup extra-virgin olive oil
½ cup grated Parmesan
    cheese
1 teaspoon salt
½ teaspoon ground black
    pepper

Garnish:

1 cup Parmesan cheese,
    grated (optional)
¼ cup pine nuts, lightly
    toasted (optional)

Homemade pesto sings of summer. This simple blend of fresh basil, garlic, rich and fruity extra-virgin olive oil, cheese, and nuts blossoms into a full-flavored coating that turns pasta from simple to spectacular. Make a more distinctive pesto by quickly blanching the garlic to cut its bitterness and by toasting the nuts to add depth to their flavor. For stronger flavor, use basil-infused oil. Make extra pesto in season to store in your freezer and you can enjoy this favorite all year.

Cooking Time: 30 minutes or less
Serves: 4

1. In a large pot over high heat, put the water up to boil for the pasta.
2. When the water is boiling, blanch the garlic for 30 to 45 seconds. (For easy blanching, skewer the garlic or use a mesh spoon to scoop it out). Rinse the garlic under cold water and pat dry. Set aside.
3. Add the pasta and cook for 7 to 11 minutes, or until al dente. Drain, reserving 2 to 3 tablespoons of pasta water.
4. Meanwhile, in a food processor fitted with a metal chopping blade, with the motor running, add the reserved garlic and purée. Add the basil and nuts and process to combine. With the motor running, slowly

Vegetarian

pour the oil down the feed tube. Scrape down the sides of the bowl. Add the cheese, salt, and pepper and process to combine.

5. In the serving bowl, combine the pasta, reserved pasta water, and pesto. Top with the cheese and nuts.

· · · · · · · · · · · · · · · · ·

Variation:

Pasta with Shrimp and Pesto: *Add ½ pound of peeled and deveined shrimp in step 3 before adding the pasta. Cook the shrimp for 1 to 2 minutes, or until just cooked through. Remove to the serving bowl.*

· · · · · · · · · · · · · · · · ·

Pasta with Tomatoes, Basil, and Garlic

5 cups coarsely chopped ripe
    tomatoes, juice
    reserved
⅓ cup extra-virgin olive oil
1 teaspoon balsamic vinegar
    (optional)
1 tablespoon salt
1 teaspoon ground black
    pepper
2 cloves garlic, peeled
¾ pound spaghetti, linguine,
    or other pasta
1 cup packed coarsely
    chopped fresh basil
½ cup grated Parmesan
    cheese

This pasta pays homage to summer's most winning combination—ripe and luscious fresh tomatoes and fragrant basil. This combination, so good in so many dishes, is simply outstanding when combined with pasta, extra-virgin olive oil, and garlic. Do not attempt this out of season. Hothouse tomatoes are simply no match for the juicy boys of summer.

Cooking Time: 30 minutes or less
Serves: 4

1. In a large pot over high heat, put the water up to boil for the pasta.
2. In the serving bowl, combine the tomatoes and their juice, oil, vinegar, salt, and pepper. Set aside.
3. When the water is boiling, blanch the garlic for 30 to 45 seconds. (For easy blanching, skewer the garlic or use a mesh spoon to scoop it out). Rinse the garlic under cold water, pat dry, mince, and add to the serving bowl.
4. Add the pasta to the pot and cook for 7 to 11 minutes, or until al dente.
5. Drain the pasta, add to the serving bowl, and stir to combine. Add the basil and stir again. Top with the Parmesan cheese.

Vegetarian

. . . .

Variation:

Pasta with Shrimp, Tomatoes, and Basil: *Add ½ pound of peeled and deveined shrimp in step 4 before adding the pasta. Cook the shrimp for 1 to 2 minutes, or until just cooked through. Remove to the serving bowl.*

. . . .

Pasta with Broccoli, Garlic, and Toasted Walnuts

⅓ cup extra-virgin olive oil
10 large cloves garlic, peeled and smashed
½ teaspoon red pepper flakes (optional)
6 cups broccoli florets
¾ pound ziti or other pasta
1 tablespoon butter
2 teaspoons salt
½ teaspoon ground black pepper
½ cup grated Parmesan cheese
1 cup coarsely chopped walnuts, lightly toasted

After its humiliation during the Bush administration, broccoli has come back with a vengeance. There are few vegetables as healthful and as tasty as this versatile cruciferous plant, especially when it's flavored with garlic, extra-virgin olive oil, and Parmesan cheese. While many pasta dishes utilize the summer's harvest, broccoli is a wonderful winter alternative. The longer the garlic and oil can stand, the stronger the taste will be. If you have bottled garlic-flavored oil, use that instead of making your own. When cooking both vegetables and pasta in the same pot, it is helpful to have a pasta set with a removable insert. Otherwise, a strainer with a long handle will do.

Cooking Time: 30 minutes or less
Serves: 4

1. In the serving bowl, combine the oil, garlic, and red pepper flakes. Set aside.
2. In a large pot over high heat, put the water up to boil for the pasta.
3. When the water is boiling, add the broccoli and cook for 4 to 6 minutes, or until crisp-tender. Remove to the serving bowl.

4. Add the pasta and cook for 9 to 11 minutes, or until al dente. Drain, reserving 2 to 3 tablespoons of pasta water.
5. Remove the garlic from the oil and discard garlic. Add the pasta, reserved pasta water, butter, salt, and pepper to the serving bowl and stir to combine. Top with the Parmesan cheese and walnuts.

· · · · · · · · · · · · · · · ·

Variation:

Pasta with Shrimp and Broccoli: *Add ½ pound of peeled and deveined shrimp in step 4 before adding the pasta. Cook the shrimp for 1 to 2 minutes, or until just cooked through. Remove to the serving bowl.*

· · · · · · · · · · · · · · · ·

Cheese Pizza

Pizza Dough:

1 cup very warm water (about 110 degrees)

1 package (2½ teaspoons) active dry yeast

3 cups flour (all-purpose, bread, or a combination)

1 teaspoon salt

2 tablespoons olive oil, plus extra for greasing the bowl

1 to 2 tablespoons cornmeal (optional for sprinkling)

Toppings:

⅔ cup pizza, pasta, or other sauce

½ pound mozzarella cheese, grated or shredded

½ cup grated Parmesan cheese

It would be unconscionable to exclude America's greatest fast food in a book about quick and easy family dinners that require only one pot or pan. Pizza is the quintessential family meal. This dough takes less than five minutes to make in a food processor and can be left to rise in the refrigerator while you are at work; but if time is short, use store-bought dough or a 12-inch Boboli. Be adventurous with toppings. Here are some suggestions: Substitute tomato sauce with ripe tomatoes, roasted garlic paste, pesto, or tapenade; replace some or all of the mozzarella cheese with goat, Fontina, or Gorgonzola cheese; experiment adding different vegetables and herbs, including mushrooms, red onions, artichoke hearts, slivered garlic, bell peppers, olives, spinach, red pepper flakes, and fresh basil. Meat lovers should add deli salami, prosciutto, or ham or recycle leftover sausage, hamburger, or chicken.

Cooking Time: 30 minutes or less
Serves: 4

1. Prepare the dough: In a food processor fitted with a metal chopping blade, sprinkle the yeast over warm water and let it stand for 5 minutes to dissolve. Add the flour, salt, and oil and process until the dough

Vegetarian

forms a ball and cleans the sides of the bowl, 20 to 30 seconds. The dough will be slightly sticky.

2. Transfer the dough to a lightly oiled large bowl and rotate to coat all sides. Cover the bowl with plastic wrap or a clean cloth and leave it to double in size, 45 minutes to 1 hour, or place it in the refrigerator for 4 or more hours.

3. When the dough has risen, preheat the oven to 450 degrees. If you have a pizza stone, top it with the cornmeal and put it in the oven for preheating; if not, lightly coat a baking sheet or pizza pan with the cornmeal and set aside.

4. Turn the dough out onto a lightly floured surface. Punch down and knead briefly to deflate the air bubbles. Let the dough rest for 15 minutes.

5. Roll or stretch the dough on a lightly floured surface until it measures 12 inches in diameter. Transfer the dough to the pizza stone, baking sheet, or pizza pan.

6. Top with the sauce, cheeses, and any additional toppings.

7. Bake for 15 to 20 minutes, or until the edges and bottom are browned and the cheese has melted.

Bean and Cheese Enchiladas in Green Sauce

12 6-inch corn tortillas
1 15-ounce container ricotta
    cheese
1½ pounds Monterey Jack, or
    cheddar cheese, grated
    or shredded
4 cups tomatillo (green) salsa,
    or taco sauce
1 4-ounce can diced green
    chiles, drained
2 15¼-ounce cans black
    beans, rinsed and
    drained
¼ cup chopped scallions
¼ cup chopped fresh cilantro
    (optional)

Mexican-style food lends itself to one-pot dishes because it efficiently and deliciously combines proteins, carbohydrates, and fiber. This simple casserole combines two cheeses, black beans, and tomatillo salsa. Tomatillos are a green, firm tomato-like fruit grown mostly in Mexico and Southern California. Covered by a thin, papery husk, they are sometimes called Chinese lantern plants. Tomatillos are tart when eaten raw, but have a fresh, lemony flavor when cooked. As with other Mexican entrées, have extra salsa, sour cream, and guacamole on hand for toppings. If tomatillo salsa is unavailable, tomato salsa can be substituted.

Cooking Time: 30 minutes or less
Serves: 4 to 6

1. Preheat the oven to 350 degrees.
2. Wrap the tortillas in aluminum foil and place in the oven to warm for 10 minutes. (Tortillas can also be wrapped in a damp towel and warmed in the microwave on high for 15 to 30 seconds).
3. In a large bowl, combine the ricotta, 4 cups of the Monterey Jack cheese, 1 cup of tomatillo sauce, chiles, black beans, scallions, and cilantro. Set aside.

Vegetarian

4. In a 13 × 9 × 2-inch baking pan, spread 1 cup of tomatillo salsa over the bottom of the dish.

5. Spoon ½ cup of filling into the center of a warmed tortilla. Roll up the tortilla to enclose the filling. Place the filled tortillas, seam side down, into the baking dish. Repeat with the remaining tortillas and filling, placing the tortillas close together and along the side of the pan to fit them all. Top with the remaining sauce and cheese.

6. Bake uncovered for 25 to 30 minutes, or until the enchiladas are heated through.

Tomato and Basil Frittata

1 tablespoon butter
¼ cup minced shallots
8 eggs
1 cup seeded and chopped
    ripe tomatoes
¼ cup coarsely chopped fresh
    basil
1 teaspoon salt
¼ teaspoon ground black
    pepper
¼ pound goat cheese,
    crumbled
2 tablespoons grated
    Parmesan cheese

Come August, if your garden is like mine, basil grows wild with aromatic wonder and ruby red tomatoes weigh down vines climbing toward the heavens. This open-faced omelet celebrates the abundance of summertime garden treasures. Frittatas are perfect for a simple dinner, savored on a blistering evening, or as a light meal after a heavy lunch. Be sure to use the ripest, most flavorful tomatoes you can find. I recommend using a non-stick pan, which allows the frittata to be easily moved during cooking.

Cooking Time: 30 minutes or less
Serves: 4

1. Preheat the oven to 350 degrees.
2. In a 10- or 11-inch nonstick, ovenproof skillet over medium-high heat, add the butter. Sauté the shallots until softened, 3 to 5 minutes, stirring frequently.
3. Meanwhile, in a medium bowl, beat the eggs. Add the tomatoes, basil, salt, and pepper. Gently add the goat cheese.

4. Reduce the heat to medium. Pour the egg mixture on top of the shallots. Cook without stirring for 1 minute, or until the eggs are almost set on the bottom. Continue cooking, using a spatula to lift the edges of the frittata toward the center of the skillet, while gently tilting the pan so the uncooked eggs run underneath the bottom of the frittata. Cook for 30 to 40 seconds and repeat the process several times until the egg on top is still wet, but not runny.
5. Sprinkle the Parmesan cheese on top of the frittata.
6. Place in the oven. Bake for 3 to 7 minutes, or until the top is just set. Do not overcook.
7. Remove from the oven, run a spatula around the skillet edge to loosen the frittata, and slide or invert it onto a serving plate.

Lentil-Vegetable Soup

2 tablespoons olive oil or
    vegetable oil
2 cups coarsely chopped
    onions
1 cup coarsely chopped
    carrots
½ cup coarsely chopped celery
1½ cups dried lentils
8 cups vegetable broth or
    reduced-sodium
    chicken broth
1 28-ounce can diced
    tomatoes
1 teaspoon dried thyme
1 cup dry white wine
1 teaspoon salt
½ teaspoon ground black
    pepper

Lentils, one of the quickest-cooking dried legumes, date back to the ancient Greeks and Romans. Because lentils don't need to be presoaked, this soup can be prepared with little notice. I like to top the soup with a sprinkling of Parmesan or cheddar cheese.

Cooking Time: 60 minutes or less
Serves: 4

1. In a large stock pot over medium heat, add the oil. Sauté the onions, carrots, and celery until softened, 5 to 8 minutes, stirring frequently.
2. Add the lentils, broth, tomatoes and their juice, and thyme and stir to combine. Bring to a boil.
3. Reduce the heat, cover, and simmer for 40 to 45 minutes, or until the lentils are tender, stirring occasionally.
4. Add the wine, salt, and pepper, stir to combine, and cook for 5 minutes.

Vegetarian

Butternut Squash and Apple Soup

This soup reminds me of the best of autumn: the plentiful squash that line the vines around Halloween and the trees weighed down with apples waiting to be picked and transformed into pies, crisps, and this wonderful soup.

Cooking Time: 60 minutes or less
Serves: 4

1. In a large stock pot over medium heat, add the butter. Add the onions and cook until softened, 3 to 5 minutes, stirring frequently. Add the ginger, cinnamon, and nutmeg and stir to combine.
2. Add the squash, apples, and broth and stir to combine. Bring to a boil.
3. Reduce the heat, cover, and simmer for 20 to 30 minutes, or until the squash is very tender, stirring occasionally.
4. In a food processor fitted with a metal chopping blade, purée the soup. (You may need to do this in two or more batches).
5. Return the soup to the pot and add ½ cup of the apple juice. Stir to combine and heat through. Season with salt and pepper. If the soup is too thick, add the remaining apple juice to achieve the desired consistency.

2 tablespoons butter
1 cup finely chopped onions
1 teaspoon ground ginger
½ teaspoon ground cinnamon
½ teaspoon ground nutmeg
7 cups peeled, seeded, and coarsely chopped butternut squash
2 cups peeled, cored, and coarsely chopped Granny Smith apples
3 cups vegetable broth, or reduced-sodium chicken broth
½ to 1 cup apple juice
1 teaspoon salt
½ teaspoon ground black pepper

Ratatouille

¼ cup olive oil
2 cups cleaned and thinly
   sliced leeks (white part
   only)
1 cup seeded and coarsely
   chopped green bell
   peppers
1 cup seeded and coarsely
   chopped red bell
   peppers
1 tablespoon minced garlic
4 cups 1-inch-cubed eggplant
1½ cups sliced zucchini
1 28-ounce can diced
   tomatoes
1 teaspoon salt
1 bay leaf
½ cup rinsed and drained
   canned chickpeas
2 tablespoons thinly sliced
   fresh basil (optional)
¼ pound cheddar cheese,
   grated or shredded

This hearty vegetable stew originated in the Provençe region of France. It's loaded with the bounty of the summer harvest: zucchini, eggplant, bell peppers, and fresh basil. To provide a little extra protein, I add some chickpeas and cheddar cheese. Many cooks top the stew with eggs and briefly bake it.

Cooking Time: 60 minutes or less
Serves: 4

1. In a large stock pot over medium heat, add the oil. Sauté the leeks, both bell peppers, and garlic until softened, 5 to 8 minutes, stirring frequently.
2. Add the eggplant and cook for 10 minutes, stirring frequently. Add the zucchini and cook for 5 minutes, stirring frequently.
3. Add the tomatoes and their juice, salt, bay leaf, and chickpeas and stir to combine.
4. Reduce the heat, cover, and simmer for 30 minutes, or until the vegetables are tender, stirring occasionally.
5. Sprinkle with the basil and cheddar cheese.

Black Bean and Butternut Squash Chili

Here's a chili, loaded with spices, beans, and veggies. It's a welcome treat on a chilly evening, and it's also great reheated the next day. Feel free to adjust the spices to get the proper amount of fire. Don't forget the toppings and chips, warm tortillas, or cornbread to complete the meal.

Cooking Time: 60 minutes or less
Serves: 4

1. In a large stock pot over medium heat, add the oil. Add the onions, red peppers, and jalapeños and sauté until softened, 5 to 8 minutes, stirring frequently.
2. Add the garlic and cook for 1 minute, stirring constantly.
3. Add the squash, broth, tomatoes and their juice, black beans, chili powder, cumin, oregano, and salt and stir to combine. Bring to a boil.
4. Reduce the heat, cover, and simmer for 30 minutes, stirring occasionally.
5. Add the corn and cook for 5 to 10 minutes, or until the vegetables are tender, stirring occasionally.
6. Top each serving with cheese and sour cream.

2 tablespoons vegetable oil
2 cups coarsely chopped onions
1 cup seeded and coarsely chopped red bell peppers
1 tablespoon seeded and finely chopped fresh jalapeño peppers
2 teaspoons minced garlic
5 cups peeled, seeded, and cubed butternut squash
1 cup vegetable broth or reduced-sodium chicken broth
1 14½-ounce can diced tomatoes
1 15¼-ounce can black beans, rinsed and drained
2 tablespoons chili powder
2 teaspoons ground cumin
1 teaspoon dried oregano
1 teaspoon salt
1 cup fresh or frozen corn
¼ pound cheddar or Monterey Jack cheese, grated or shredded (optional)
4 tablespoons sour cream (optional)

Eggplant and Vegetable Tian

1 large red onion, thinly sliced
(about 10 ounces)
5 tablespoons olive oil
2 teaspoons salt
1 teaspoon dried thyme
1 medium eggplant, thinly
sliced (about ¾ pound)
1 medium yellow squash or
zucchini, thinly sliced
(about ⅓ pound)
2 large ripe tomatoes, thinly
sliced (about 1 pound)
¼ cup chopped fresh basil
½ pound goat cheese,
crumbled
¼ cup bread crumbs,
homemade or
packaged
2 tablespoons grated
Parmesan cheese

A tian is both the name of a casserole cooked in a shallow clay pot as well as the name of the pot itself. This vegetarian specialty is found primarily in the Provençe region of France. This tian features hearty eggplant, summer squash, red onions, tomatoes, and goat cheese, but you can adapt it to show off whatever is plentiful in your garden or at the farmers' market.

Cooking Time: 60 minutes or less
Serves: 4 to 6

1. Preheat the oven to 350 degrees.
2. In a large shallow decorative ovenproof dish, or a 13 × 9 × 2-inch baking pan, arrange the onions in a single layer. Drizzle with 1 tablespoon of the oil, ½ teaspoon salt, and ¼ teaspoon thyme. Top with a layer of the eggplant slices. Drizzle with 1 tablespoon of oil, ½ teaspoon salt, and ¼ teaspoon thyme. Top with a layer of the squash slices. Drizzle with 1 tablespoon of oil, ½ teaspoon salt, and ¼ teaspoon thyme. Top with the tomato slices. Drizzle with 1 tablespoon of oil, ½ teaspoon salt, and ¼ teaspoon thyme.

3. Cover with aluminum foil and bake for 45 minutes. Remove the foil, sprinkle with the basil and goat cheese, and drizzle with the remaining tablespoon of oil. Top with the bread crumbs and Parmesan cheese. Bake uncovered for 10 to 15 minutes, or until the cheese has melted. For added browning, place under the broiler for 1 to 2 minutes.

4. Remove from the oven. Cover with aluminum foil and let stand for 10 minutes before serving.

Chile Relleno Phyllo Bake

3 eggs
½ pound cream cheese, room temperature
1 cup ricotta cheese
2 7-ounce cans whole green chiles, drained
¼ cup coarsely chopped fresh cilantro (optional)
¼ cup thinly sliced scallions
½ pound cheddar cheese, grated or shredded
½ cup (1 stick) butter, melted or very soft
12 sheets phyllo dough, defrosted and cut in half widthwise
2 cups fresh tomato salsa, ready-made or recipe, page 175 (optional)

Creamy chile-studded custard is spread between layers of buttery phyllo dough in this dressed-up version of the classic Mexican dish. Ready-made phyllo dough (also known as filo or fillo), tissue-paper thin sheets of pastry, makes a distinctively crispy and light crust. It does take patience to work with phyllo, as it is fragile and crumbles easily; but because multiple layers are used, mistakes are invisible to the eye and palate. A salad of shredded lettuce, chopped tomatoes, jicama, grapefruit slices, and avocado in a creamy citrus vinaigrette is a nice accompaniment.

Cooking Time: 60 minutes or less
Serves: 4

1. Preheat the oven to 350 degrees.
2. In a food processor fitted with a metal chopping blade, combine the eggs, cream cheese, and ricotta. Add the chiles, cilantro, scallions, and cheddar cheese and pulse to combine. (This can also be mixed in a large bowl).

Vegetarian

3. Lightly butter the bottom and sides of a $13 \times 9 \times 2$-inch baking pan. Cover with 7 sheets of the phyllo, brushing each sheet with butter before adding the next.

4. Spread half of the cheese mixture on top of the phyllo. Top with 7 sheets of phyllo, brushing each sheet with butter before adding the next. Top with the remaining cheese mixture. Top with 10 layers of phyllo, brushing each sheet with butter before adding the next. Lightly brush the top sheet with butter.

5. Bake for 45 minutes, or until lightly browned and cooked through. Let stand for 5 minutes before serving.

Spinach and Ricotta Lasagna

1 15-ounce container ricotta
cheese
3 cups coarsely chopped
spinach leaves
1 cup finely chopped fresh
basil
½ to 1 teaspoon red pepper
flakes (optional)
4 cups prepared pasta sauce
1 cup water
½ pound lasagna noodles
1 pound mozzarella cheese,
grated or shredded
1½ cups grated Parmesan
cheese

Now that most lasagna noodles do not need to be precooked, making this hearty pasta dish is easier than ever. To keep the noodles from drying out, add a little water to the tomato sauce before baking. Be as creative as you want, adding more vegetables or precooked meat to the ricotta cheese filling and spicing up your pasta sauce to make this dish your own. For a fresh taste, instead of using jarred sauce, ask your favorite Italian restaurant if they sell their homemade tomato sauce.

Cooking Time: 60 minutes or less
Serves: 4 to 6

1. Preheat the oven to 350 degrees.
2. In a medium bowl, combine the ricotta, spinach, basil, and red pepper flakes.
3. In a 13 × 9 × 2-inch baking pan, mix 1 cup of the pasta sauce and ½ cup of the water and spread over the bottom of the pan.
4. Cover the bottom of the pan with some of lasagna noodles. You will need to overlap or break some noodles to cover the bottom completely.

Vegetarian

5. Top with half of the ricotta mixture, 1 cup of the pasta sauce, and half of the mozzarella cheese. Sprinkle with ½ cup of the Parmesan cheese.
6. Cover the cheese with another layer of noodles. Top with the remaining ricotta mixture, 2 cups of pasta sauce, and ½ cup of water.
7. Top with the remaining mozzarella and Parmesan cheeses.
8. Cover with aluminum foil and bake for 30 minutes. Check to make sure the sides are not drying out. If necessary, pour a few tablespoons of water or sauce into the corners.
9. Uncover and bake for 15 to 25 minutes, or until the lasagna is heated through and the cheese is bubbly. Let stand for 5 to 10 minutes before serving.

Tomato, Goat Cheese, and Pesto Tart

Crust:

1¼ cups all-purpose flour
¼ teaspoon salt
½ cup (1 stick) unsalted but-
      ter, chilled and cut into
      ½-inch pieces
2 to 4 tablespoons ice water

Filling:

4 eggs
1 cup cream or milk
1 cup milk
½ cup pesto, ready-made or
      recipe, page 114
½ teaspoon salt
½ teaspoon ground black
      pepper
¼ pound goat cheese,
      crumbled
2 medium red, orange, and/or
      yellow ripe tomatoes,
      thinly sliced (about ½
      pound)

> *Creamy goat cheese mingles with basil pesto and fresh tomatoes in this delightful tart. It tastes and looks like summertime, with vibrant colors and vivid flavors. Search your farmers' market to find yellow or orange tomatoes to add to its colorful presentation. Make your own crust or buy a ready-made crust and fit it into a 9-inch pie plate.*

Cooking Time: 60 minutes or less
Serves: 4

1. Prepare the crust: In a food processor fitted with a metal chopping blade, mix the flour and salt (5 seconds). Add the butter and pulse until the mixture resembles coarse meal (10 short pulses). Sprinkle the minimum amount of water over the mixture and pulse until distributed throughout the dough and the crumbs start sticking together (5 to 10 pulses). Process just until the dough holds together, adding the remaining water if necessary. Do not allow the dough to form a ball.

2. Scrape the dough onto the work surface. Shape the dough into a 1-inch-thick disc. Wrap the dough tightly with plastic wrap and refrigerate for 30 minutes, or until it is firm enough to roll out.

3. Preheat the oven to 450 degrees.

4. Roll out the dough and fit into a 9-inch pie pan. Prick the dough with a fork and bake for 5 to 10 minutes, or until lightly browned. Remove from the oven and reduce the temperature to 350 degrees.

5. Prepare the filling: Meanwhile, in a medium bowl, beat the eggs, cream, milk, pesto, salt, and pepper. Set aside.

6. Line the partially baked pie crust with the goat cheese. Add the egg mixture.

7. Bake for 30 minutes, or until just set. Top with the tomatoes, placed in slightly overlapping concentric circles. Bake for 10 to 20 minutes, or until the eggs are set and the center doesn't jiggle. If the crust begins to brown before the tart is ready, cover it with aluminum foil to prevent burning. Let stand 5 to 10 minutes before serving.

6
WEEKEND COOKING

Poultry

Chicken Wings and
  Meatballs

Coq au Vin

Roasted Chicken with
  Vegetables

Rock Cornish Game Hens
  Stuffed with Couscous

Meat

Lamb Stew

Beef Bourguignon

Osso Buco

Beef Stew

Lamb Shanks and White
  Beans

Split Pea and Ham Soup

New Mexico Pork and
  Green Chile Stew

Hungarian Goulash

Sweet and Sour Meatballs
  with Sauerkraut

Vegetarian

Mushroom-Barley Soup

Black Bean Soup

As working moms, weekends are our time to kick back, relax, and enjoy our children. With the week behind us, and two days full of the promise of freedom (and errands, and errands, and errands), Saturday and Sunday let us reclaim our lives, set our own schedules, and move at our own pace.

During this brief reprieve from being perpetually hurried and harried, meal preparation takes on a more leisurely nature. We can enjoy recipes that require longer cooking times, thus liberating ourselves from last minute scurrying. Instead of the usual rush to get something on the table, these meals permit us to start dinner in advance. We can put our feet up and enjoy a stress-free period before eating, while savoring the tantalizing aromas that presage the promise of something wonderful to come.

These meals, reminiscent of childhood Sunday dinners, allow time for hearty stews to gently bubble away on the stove, infusing gravy and vegetables with gusto while slowly tenderizing morsels of meat. Roasted chicken becomes crackley crisp, golden, and juicy. Healthful bean and vegetable soups blossom as flavors bloom and the legumes ready their nutritious goodness.

Weekends are also the perfect time to anticipate our needs for the coming week and lay the groundwork for weekday dinners. Whether we prepare an extra meal to serve later, double a recipe to store in the freezer, or simply chop extra vegetables to use later, we'll find a little planning goes a long way towards future peace of mind!

Chicken Wings and Meatballs

This dish was a childhood standard in my house. It's fun for kids with tiny fingers to pick up the chicken wings and tiny meatballs and get down and dirty enjoying this dish.

Cooking Time: Over 60 minutes
Serves: 4

1. In a medium bowl, soak the bread in milk until saturated. Squeeze the milk from the bread and discard the excess liquid. Mash the bread with the beef. Form small meatballs, 1 to 1½ inches in diameter. Set aside.

2. In a large skillet over medium-high heat, add the oil. Brown the chicken on all sides, 3 to 5 minutes. (You may need to do this in two or more batches). Remove the chicken and reserve.

3. Discard any fat from the skillet. Add the soup, water, Italian seasoning, salt, and pepper and stir to combine. Bring to a boil.

4. Return the chicken to the pot. Top with the meatballs. Reduce the heat, cover, and simmer for 1 hour, stirring occasionally.

5. Add the potatoes and onions and cook for 20 to 25 minutes. Add the peas and cook for 1 to 2 minutes.

1 slice white bread, crust removed
¼ cup milk
1 pound lean ground beef or ground turkey
2 tablespoons vegetable oil
2 pounds chicken wings or wing drumettes, trimmed of excess skin
1 8-ounce can tomato soup
1 cup water
2 teaspoons Italian seasoning
1 teaspoon salt
½ teaspoon ground black pepper
8 small new potatoes, quartered if large (about 1 pound)
8 pearl or boiling onions, peeled
1 cup fresh or frozen peas

Coq au Vin

¼ pound bacon, coarsely
    chopped
1 3- to 4-pound chicken, cut
    into 8 pieces
8 pearl or boiling onions,
    peeled
2 cups small mushrooms,
    halved if large
3 tablespoons all-purpose flour
2 teaspoons minced garlic
1 teaspoon dried thyme
2 cups Burgundy or dry red
    wine
1 cup reduced-sodium
    chicken broth
12 baby carrots, or 2 cups
    sliced carrots (1-inch-
    thick pieces)
12 small new potatoes,
    quartered if large
    (about 1½ pounds)

This aromatic chicken stew celebrates the cuisine of the Burgundy region of France and its coveted export, the dry full-bodied wines of the region. This one-pot meal can be prepared the night before, refrigerated, and then placed in the oven the next day for its final cooking. For a modern twist on this classic dish, experiment by using exotic mushrooms like shiitakes or portobellos instead of domestic button mushrooms. Make sure to serve lots of crusty bread so you don't miss a single drop.

Cooking Time: Over 60 minutes
Serves: 4

1. In a large stock pot or skillet over medium-high heat, sauté the bacon until brown and crisp, 8 to 10 minutes, stirring frequently. Transfer the bacon to paper towels, using a slotted spoon.
2. Add the chicken and brown, 3 to 5 minutes per side. Remove the chicken and reserve. (You may need to do this in two or more batches).
3. Discard all but 2 tablespoons of fat from the pot. Add the onions and mushrooms. Cook until browned, 8 to 10 minutes, stirring occasionally. Do not overcrowd the pot.

4. Add the flour, garlic, and thyme and cook for 1 to 2 minutes, stirring constantly.

5. Add the wine and broth. Bring to a boil and stir to deglaze and dislodge any bits of food that have stuck to the bottom of the pot.

6. Return the bacon and chicken to the pot. (If desired, refrigerate overnight at this point). Add the carrots and potatoes.

7. Reduce the heat, cover, and simmer for 1 hour, or until the chicken is cooked through and the vegetables are tender, basting with the cooking liquid and turning the chicken occasionally.

Roasted Chicken with Vegetables

1 3- to 4-pound chicken, giblets, excess fat, and excess skin removed
1 lemon, halved
2 tablespoons butter, melted or very soft
1 tablespoon dried rosemary
1 tablespoon salt
½ teaspoon ground black pepper
10 cloves garlic, peeled
4 large carrots, halved lengthwise and cut into 2-inch pieces (about 1 pound)
3 large onions, peeled and quartered (about 2¼ pounds)
3 large celery stalks, trimmed and cut into 2-inch pieces (about ½ pound)
8 small new potatoes, quartered if large (about 1 pound)
2 sweet potatoes, halved lengthwise and cut into 2-inch pieces (about 1 pound)
2 tablespoons olive oil
1 cup reduced-sodium chicken broth

This time-honored dinner will warm hearts, appetites, and kitchens on a cold winter's night. After a short prep, all you have to do is wait for its intoxicating aroma to overtake your home. For added browning, flip the chicken midway through cooking. Whether it's a family meal or a guests-only dinner party, no one ever outgrows this favorite.

Cooking Time: Over 60 minutes
Serves: 4

1. Preheat the oven to 450 degrees.
2. Let the chicken stand at room temperature for 30 minutes before cooking.
3. Rub the chicken with one lemon half and then lightly coat with the butter. Sprinkle with the rosemary, salt, and pepper.
4. Place the chicken in a large roasting pan on a vertical roaster or a V-shaped rack. Surround the chicken with the garlic, carrots, onions, celery, potatoes, and sweet potatoes. Drizzle the oil, juice from the remaining lemon half, and broth over the vegetables and toss to combine.
5. Roast the chicken for 20 minutes.
6. Reduce the heat to 350 degrees and stir the vegetables. Bake for 1¼ to 1½ hours, until the chicken is cooked through, stirring the vegetables every 30 minutes. The chicken is ready when a meat thermometer

inserted into the inner thigh registers between 170 and 180 degrees and juices run clear, not pink.

7. Remove the pan from the oven and let the chicken rest for 10 to 15 minutes.

8. Carve or cut the chicken into pieces and serve with the vegetables.

. . . .

Variation:

Herbed Roast Chicken: *For added flavor and a dramatic presentation, loosen the skin around the breast and insert fresh herbs (rosemary, thyme, and sage are all nice additions) or slivers of garlic.*

. . . .

Rock Cornish Game Hens Stuffed with Couscous

Stuffing:

1 cup reduced-sodium
    chicken broth
1 cup peeled, cored, and
    finely chopped apples
⅔ cup couscous
3 tablespoons currants, or
    raisins
1 teaspoon lemon zest
1 teaspoon salt
¼ cup pine nuts, lightly
    toasted

Hens:

4 1-pound Cornish game
    hens, or 2 larger hens,
    giblets, excess fat, and
    excess skin removed
1 tablespoon butter, melted or
    very soft
1 tablespoon dried thyme
1 teaspoon salt
½ teaspoon ground black pepper
2 large onions, peeled and quar-
    tered (about 1½ pounds)
2 large carrots, halved
    lengthwise and cut
    into 2-inch pieces
    (about ½ pound)
2 cups Brussels sprouts, trimmed
    and halved (optional)
2 tablespoons olive oil
¼ to ½ cup reduced-sodium
    chicken broth
2 cups trimmed green beans

Rock Cornish game hens, an American crossbreed between white Plymouth Rock hens and Cornish gamecocks, are a nice departure from traditional chicken dinners. They are elegant when presented, yet their preparation is not demanding. Most Cornish hens are between five and six weeks old, weigh around one to two pounds, and have less fat and calories than older chickens. These are stuffed with fruity couscous and then roasted alongside vegetables. When cooking a stuffed bird, add 15 minutes to the cooking time.

Cooking Time: Over 60 minutes
Serves: 4

1. Preheat the oven to 450 degrees.
2. Prepare the stuffing: In a microwave, bring the broth to a boil.
3. In a medium bowl, combine the apples, couscous, currants, lemon zest, and salt. Pour in the broth. Cover with aluminum foil and let stand for 5 to 10 minutes, or until the broth is absorbed. Add the pine nuts and toss to combine. Set aside.
4. Prepare the hens: Rub the hens with the butter and sprinkle with the thyme, salt, and pepper.
5. Loosely stuff each hen with between ⅓ and ½ cup of the couscous mixture. Tie the legs together at the ankles with kitchen string to secure.

6. In a large roasting pan or on a rack in a large roasting pan, place the hens. Surround the hens with the onions, carrots, and Brussels sprouts. Drizzle the oil and ¼ cup broth over the vegetables and toss to combine.
7. Roast the hens for 20 minutes.
8. Reduce the heat to 350 degrees. Add the green beans and stir the vegetables to combine. If the vegetables begin to dry out, add another ¼ cup broth.
9. Bake for 30 to 40 minutes for 1-pound birds, or 55 to 65 minutes for larger birds, or until the hens are cooked through, stirring the vegetables every 30 minutes. The hens are ready when a meat thermometer inserted into the thigh registers between 170 and 180 degrees and juices run clear, not pink.
10. Remove the pan from the oven and let the hens rest for 5 to 10 minutes. If serving larger birds, cut them in half. Serve with the stuffing and vegetables.

Lamb Stew

2 tablespoons butter
1½ pounds boneless lamb
    shoulder or stew meat,
    cut into 1½-inch
    pieces
2 tablespoons all-purpose flour
2 cups reduced-sodium beef
    broth
12 pearl or boiling onions,
    peeled
12 small new potatoes,
    quartered if large
    (about 1½ pounds)
12 baby carrots, or 2 cups
    sliced carrots (1-inch
    pieces)
1 cup turnips, peeled and cut
    into 1-inch pieces
    (optional)
1 teaspoon dried thyme
½ teaspoon dried rosemary
½ teaspoon dried sage
    (optional)
1 bay leaf
2 cups trimmed and cut green
    beans
1 teaspoon salt
½ teaspoon ground black
    pepper

Lamb stew is actually a classic French dish named navarin printanier, *or "spring lamb," because it is most frequently made in the spring when lambs are young, tender, and flavorful. Lamb is braised and then baked with baby vegetables until the stew's flavor becomes something greater than its individual ingredients. This recipe was given to me my mother, Bert Hoberman.*

Cooking Time: Over 60 minutes
Serves: 4

1. Preheat the oven to 350 degrees.
2. In a large ovenproof stock pot over medium-high heat, add the butter. Brown the lamb on all sides, 3 to 5 minutes. Do not overcrowd the meat. (You may need to do this in two or more batches).
3. Add the flour and stir until it is absorbed into the meat, 1 to 2 minutes.
4. Add the broth. Bring to a boil and stir to deglaze and dislodge any bits of lamb that have stuck to the bottom of the pot and to incorporate the flour. Scrape your stirring spoon to free any flour that has adhered to it.

5. Add the onions, potatoes, carrots, turnips, thyme, rosemary, sage, and bay leaf. The liquid will just barely cover the stew. Cover and place in the oven. After 10 to 15 minutes, check to make sure the stew is gently simmering. If necessary, adjust the oven temperature to correct.

6. Bake for 1¼ hours. Add the green beans and bake for 15 minutes, or until the meat and vegetables are tender.

7. Remove from the oven and skim off any fat. Season with salt and pepper.

Beef Bourguignon

¼ pound bacon, coarsely chopped
1½ pounds boneless beef chuck, cut into 1½-inch pieces
2 teaspoons salt
½ teaspoon ground black pepper
1 tablespoon all-purpose flour
16 pearl or boiling onions, peeled
2 cups sliced carrots (1-inch thick)
1 tablespoon minced garlic
1½ cups reduced-sodium beef broth
¼ cup Cognac (optional)
2 cups Burgundy or dry red wine
2 cups small mushrooms, halved if large
1 teaspoon dried thyme

This enticing classic hails from the Burgundy region of France. Hearty beef, onions, carrots, and mushrooms are slowly simmered in a luscious red wine sauce for a truly succulent stew. Don't scrimp on the wine. For optimum flavor, use a drinkable dry red that you would enjoy on its own. Make sure there's lots of crusty French bread so you won't miss a single drop of this rich, robust gravy.

Cooking Time: Over 60 minutes
Serves: 4

1. Preheat the oven to 325 degrees.
2. In a large ovenproof stock pot over medium heat, sauté the bacon until brown and crisp, 8 to 10 minutes, stirring frequently. Transfer the bacon to paper towels, using a slotted spoon. Set aside.
3. Sprinkle the beef with the salt and pepper and coat with the flour. Brown the beef on all sides, 3 to 5 minutes. Do not overcrowd the meat. Remove the meat and reserve in a large bowl. (You may need to do this in two or more batches).
4. Add the onions and carrots and cook until lightly browned, 5 to 8 minutes, stirring frequently.
5. Add the garlic and cook for 1 minute, stirring constantly. Transfer the vegetables to the bowl with the beef. Set aside.

Weekend Cooking

6. Add the broth and Cognac to the pot. Bring to a boil and stir to deglaze and dislodge any bits of food that have stuck to the bottom of the pot. Boil for 5 minutes, or until the broth begins to reduce.

7. Return the bacon, beef, and vegetables with their juices to the pot. Add the wine, mushrooms, and thyme. The liquid will just barely cover the stew. Cover and place in the oven. After 10 to 15 minutes, check to make sure the stew is gently simmering. If necessary, adjust the oven temperature to correct.

8. Bake for $1\frac{1}{4}$ to $1\frac{1}{2}$ hours, or until the meat and vegetables are tender.

9. Remove from the oven and skim off any fat.

Osso Buco

4 meaty veal or lamb shanks
   (about 3 pounds)
2 teaspoons salt
1 teaspoon ground black
   pepper
2 tablespoons olive oil
1 cup coarsely chopped
   onions
1 cup coarsely chopped
   carrots
¼ cup coarsely chopped celery
2 teaspoons minced garlic
1 cup reduced-sodium
   chicken broth
½ cup dry white wine
1 14½-ounce can diced
   tomatoes
2 tablespoons chopped fresh
   Italian parsley
2 teaspoons lemon zest
1 teaspoon minced garlic

Translated, the name of this northern Italian dish means "bone with a hole filled with marrow," which is a slightly crude but apt description of what makes this delicacy so popular: the flavorful bone marrow. The traditional garnish for osso buco is gremolata, a mixture of lemon zest, parsley, and garlic. While this braise is definitely a meal in itself, risotto Milanese (saffron risotto) is a traditional accompaniment. If you don't enjoy veal, you can make osso buco with lamb shanks.

Cooking Time: Over 60 minutes
Serves: 4

1. Preheat the oven to 325 degrees.
2. Sprinkle the meat with the salt and pepper.
3. In a large ovenproof skillet over medium-high heat, add the oil. Brown the shanks on all sides, 8 to 10 minutes. Do not overcrowd the meat. Remove the meat and reserve.
4. Add the onions, carrots, celery, and garlic and sauté until softened, 5 to 8 minutes, stirring frequently.
5. Add the broth, wine, and tomatoes and their juice and stir to combine. Bring to a boil and stir to deglaze and dislodge any bits of food that have stuck to the bottom of the skillet.

6. Return the shanks to the skillet and distribute them between the vegetables. Cover and place in the oven. After 10 to 15 minutes, check to make sure the stew is gently simmering. If necessary, adjust the oven temperature to correct.

7. Bake for 1¼ to 1½ hours, or until the meat and vegetables are tender, turning the shanks after 45 minutes. Remove from the oven, turn the shanks, and let stand for 5 to 10 minutes.

8. Meanwhile, prepare the gremolata. Combine the parsley, lemon zest, and garlic until blended. Sprinkle on top of the Osso Buco.

Beef Stew

2 pounds beef chuck, cut into
1½-inch pieces
1 teaspoon salt
½ teaspoon ground black
pepper
2 tablespoons vegetable oil
2 cups coarsely chopped
onions
2 teaspoons minced garlic
2 tablespoons all-purpose flour
1 cup dry red wine
1 cup reduced-sodium beef
broth
1 teaspoon dried thyme
1 bay leaf
3 cups peeled and halved new
potatoes
3 cups sliced carrots (½-inch-
thick pieces)
1 cup fresh or frozen peas
(optional)

Hearty chunks of beef are seared to caramelize and seal in flavorful juices, mixed with an aromatic assortment of vegetables, and then placed in the oven to maintain a gentle simmer. As the stew slowly cooks, the connective tissue in the beef breaks down, making the meat so tender you can cut it with a spoon. The addition of the wine, broth, and vegetables adds sublime flavor. Who says beef stew is boring?

Cooking Time: Over 60 minutes
Serves: 4

1. Preheat the oven to 275 degrees.
2. Sprinkle the beef with salt and pepper.
3. In a large ovenproof stock pot over medium-high heat, add the oil. Brown the beef on all sides, 3 to 5 minutes. Do not overcrowd the meat. Remove the meat and reserve. (You may need to do this in two or more batches).
4. Add the onions and sauté until softened, 3 to 5 minutes, stirring frequently. Reduce the heat to medium and add the garlic. Cook for 1 minute, stirring constantly.
5. Add the flour and stir until it is absorbed into the onions, 1 to 2 minutes.

6. Add the wine, broth, thyme, and bay leaf. Bring to a boil and stir to deglaze and dislodge any bits of food that have stuck to the bottom of the pot and to incorporate the flour. Scrape your stirring spoon to free any flour that has adhered to it.

7. Return the beef and its juice to the pot. The liquid will just barely cover the stew. Cover and place in the oven. After 10 to 15 minutes, check to make sure the stew is gently simmering. If necessary, adjust the oven temperature to correct.

8. Bake for 1 hour. Remove the pot from the oven. Check to make sure the broth has not evaporated. If necessary, add a little hot water. Add the potatoes and carrots, cover, and return to the oven.

9. Bake for 1 to 1½ hours, or until the meat is tender. Add the peas and bake for 1 to 2 minutes.

10. Remove from the oven and skim off any fat.

Lamb Shanks and White Beans

4 meaty lamb shanks (about 3
    pounds)
2 teaspoons salt
1 teaspoon ground black
    pepper
2 tablespoons olive oil
1 cup coarsely chopped
    onions
1 cup coarsely chopped
    carrots
1 tablespoon minced garlic
2 teaspoons dried rosemary
1 teaspoon dried thyme
1 cup dry red wine or white
    wine
1 cup reduced-sodium
    chicken broth
1 28-ounce can diced
    tomatoes
2 15-ounce cans cannellini or
    small white beans,
    rinsed and drained

Tender braised lamb is slow-cooked with creamy white beans and seasoned with rosemary and thyme for a taste sensation. This is a wonderful dish for entertaining because it can be prepared ahead of time and left on the stove while you enjoy your guests.

Cooking Time: Over 60 minutes
Serves: 4

1. Sprinkle the lamb with salt and pepper.
2. In a large skillet over medium-high heat, add the oil. Brown the lamb on all sides, 8 to 10 minutes. Do not overcrowd the meat. Remove the lamb and reserve.
3. Add the onions, carrots, garlic, rosemary, and thyme and sauté until softened, 5 to 8 minutes, stirring frequently.
4. Add the wine, broth, and tomatoes and their juice. Bring to a boil and stir to deglaze and dislodge any bits of food that have stuck to the bottom of the skillet.
5. Return the shanks to the skillet and spoon the tomatoes and liquids over the lamb.
6. Reduce the heat, cover, and simmer for 1 hour, turning the lamb shanks after 30 minutes.
7. Add the beans and cook uncovered for 45 minutes to 1 hour, or until the meat is tender and the cooking liquid thickens, stirring and turning the lamb occasionally.

Split Pea and Ham Soup

This thick and creamy soup has "comfort" written all over it. So hearty and rich with peas, veggies, and ham it is almost like a stew. For a vegetarian soup, leave out the ham and substitute vegetable broth for the chicken broth.

9 cups reduced-sodium
   chicken broth
2 cups dried split peas
1 large meaty ham bone, or ½
   pound thickly cut
   country ham, chopped
1 cup coarsely chopped
   onions
1 cup coarsely chopped
   carrots
1 cup coarsely chopped celery
½ teaspoon dried thyme
1 teaspoon salt
½ teaspoon ground black
   pepper

Cooking Time: Over 60 minutes
Serves: 4 to 6

1. In a large stock pot over high heat, combine the broth and split peas. Bring to a boil for 2 minutes. Remove from the heat, cover, and let stand for 1 hour.

2. Add the ham bone or ham, onions, carrots, celery, and thyme. Bring to a boil.

3. Reduce the heat, cover, and simmer for 1½ to 2 hours, or until the peas are tender, stirring occasionally.

4. If using a ham bone, remove it and cut the meat into bite-size pieces. Return the ham to the pot.

5. Add the salt and pepper. This soup will thicken as it stands. If necessary, add extra broth or water to achieve the desired consistency.

New Mexico Pork and Green Chile Stew

2 tablespoons vegetable oil
1½ pounds boneless pork shoulder, loin end, or butt, cut into 1-inch pieces
1½ cups chopped onions
1 tablespoon minced garlic
2 tablespoons all-purpose flour
3 cups reduced-sodium chicken broth
1 cup Mexican-style canned diced tomatoes, drained (optional)
2 teaspoons dried oregano
½ teaspoon ground cumin
2 cups thickly sliced carrots
2 cups peeled, ¾-inch-cubed potatoes
⅓ cup seeded and coarsely chopped fresh jalapeño peppers, or 1 4-ounce can green chiles, drained and chopped
1 teaspoon salt
½ teaspoon ground black pepper

From the heart of the Southwest comes this rich and fragrant stew, seasoned with green chiles, onions, and garlic. Serve it with warm tortillas or corn bread, fresh from the oven, and a salad brimming with chunks of avocado and tomato. A note of caution: When seeding and chopping fresh chiles, wear rubber gloves and keep your hands away from your eyes.

Cooking Time: Over 60 minutes
Serves: 4

1. In a large stock pot over medium-high heat, add the oil. Brown the pork on all sides, 3 to 5 minutes. Do not overcrowd the meat. Remove the meat and reserve. (You may need to do this in two or more batches).

2. Add the onions and sauté until softened, 3 to 5 minutes, stirring frequently. Reduce the heat to medium and add the garlic. Cook for 1 minute, stirring constantly.

3. Add the flour and stir until it is absorbed into the onions, 1 to 2 minutes.

4. Add the broth, tomatoes, oregano, and cumin. Bring to a boil and stir to deglaze and dislodge any bits of food that have stuck to the bottom of the pot and to incorporate the flour. Scrape your stirring spoon to free any flour that has adhered to it.

5. Return the pork and its juice to the pot, reduce the heat, cover, and simmer for 1 hour, stirring occasionally.
6. Add the carrots, potatoes, and jalapeños and cook for 20 to 30 minutes, or until the vegetables and pork are tender.
7. Remove from the oven and skim off any fat. Season with salt and pepper.

Hungarian Goulash

1 tablespoon butter
1 cup chopped onions
1 tablespoon sweet paprika
1 teaspoon minced garlic
1 teaspoon caraway seeds
1 teaspoon dill seed (optional)
¼ teaspoon marjoram
   (optional)
1½ pounds boneless beef
   chuck, cut into 1½-
   inch pieces
2 tablespoons all-purpose flour
2 cups reduced-sodium beef
   broth
2 tablespoons tomato paste
1 tablespoon Worcestershire
   sauce (optional)
2 cups peeled, 1-inch-cubed
   potatoes
1 teaspoon salt
½ teaspoon ground black
   pepper
4 tablespoons sour cream

The defining ingredient for this European stew is sweet paprika. It's worth searching out Hungarian paprika for a more authentic taste. Although the ingredient list may appear a little long, this robust favorite is easy to put together. While goulash can be served over buttered egg noodles, here it is cooked with potatoes and simply garnished with a dollop of sour cream.

Cooking Time: Over 60 minutes
Serves: 4

1. In a large stock pot over medium-high heat, add the butter. Add the onions and sauté until softened, 3 to 5 minutes, stirring frequently. Reduce the heat to medium and add the paprika, garlic, caraway seeds, dill seed, and marjoram. Cook for 1 minute, stirring constantly.
2. Add the beef and stir to combine. Cook for 2 minutes, stirring frequently.
3. Add the flour and stir until it is absorbed into the onions and beef, 1 to 2 minutes.
4. Add the broth, tomato paste, and Worcestershire sauce. Bring to a boil and stir to deglaze and dislodge any bits of food that have stuck to the bottom of the pot and to incorporate the flour. Scrape your stirring spoon to free any flour that has adhered to it.

5. Reduce the heat, cover, and simmer for 1 hour, stirring occasionally.
6. Add the potatoes, cover, and simmer for 30 to 45 minutes, or until the meat is tender, stirring occasionally. Season with salt and pepper.
7. Top each serving with 1 tablespoon of the sour cream.

Sweet and Sour Meatballs with Sauerkraut

Sauce:

1 cup chopped onions
½ cup packed brown sugar
½ cup raisins
1 15-ounce can tomato sauce
1 pound sauerkraut

Meatballs:

2 slices white bread, crusts
    removed
½ cup milk
2 pounds lean ground beef or
    ground turkey
1 cup finely chopped onions
2 tablespoons brown sugar
1 teaspoon salt
½ teaspoon ground black
    pepper
2 tablespoons vegetable oil

My husband insisted I include this favorite from his childhood. His mom had this recipe in her family for generations. With four kids to feed, one-pot meals were a standard in this busy family. Ruth sometimes served this with mashed potatoes, but it is filling on its own.

Cooking Time: Over 60 minutes
Serves: 4

1. Prepare the sauce: In a medium bowl, mix the onions, brown sugar, raisins, tomato sauce, and sauerkraut. Set aside.
2. Prepare the meatballs: In a large bowl, soak the bread in the milk until saturated. Squeeze the milk from the bread and discard the excess liquid. Mash the bread with the beef. Add the onions, brown sugar, salt, and pepper and stir to combine. Form meatballs 1½ to 2 inches in diameter.
3. In a stock pot over medium heat, add the oil. Lightly brown the meatballs on all sides, 5 to 8 minutes. (You may need to do this in two or more batches). Remove the meatballs and reserve.
4. Discard any fat from the pot. Spoon half of the sauce into the pot. Top with half of the meatballs. Repeat with the remaining sauce and meatballs.
5. Cover and simmer, stirring occasionally, for 1½ hours, or until the meat is cooked through.

Mushroom-Barley Soup

First cultivated in ancient Egypt, barley dates back to between 6000 B.C. and 5000 B.C. A popular offering to the gods, barley was found alongside other "treasures" in the tomb of King Tut. For a richer mushroom flavor, add ¼ to ½ ounce of dried porcini mushrooms that have been soaked for 30 minutes in 1 cup of the broth.

2 tablespoons vegetable oil
1 cup finely chopped onions
1 cup finely chopped carrots
½ cup finely chopped celery
1 teaspoon garlic, minced
5½ cups coarsely chopped
    mushrooms
8 cups vegetable broth or
    reduced-sodium
    chicken broth
½ cup pearl barley
1 tablespoon finely chopped
    fresh dill (optional)
1 teaspoon salt
½ teaspoon ground black
    pepper

Cooking Time: Over 60 minutes
Serves: 4

1. In a large stock pot over medium heat, add the oil. Sauté the onions, carrots, celery, and garlic until softened, 5 to 8 minutes, stirring frequently.
2. Increase the heat. Add the mushrooms and cook for 5 to 8 minutes, or until the mushrooms give off most of their liquid, stirring frequently.
3. Add the broth. Bring to a boil for 5 minutes.
4. Add the barley and stir to combine. Reduce the heat, cover, and simmer for 40 to 50 minutes, or until the barley is tender and the soup thickens, stirring occasionally.
5. Season with the dill, salt, and pepper.

Black Bean Soup

2 tablespoons olive oil or
    vegetable oil
2 cups finely chopped onions
1 cup finely chopped carrots
½ cup finely chopped celery
2 teaspoons minced garlic
2 cups dried black beans,
    soaked overnight and
    drained
8 cups vegetable broth or
    reduced-sodium
    chicken broth
2 teaspoons ground cumin

This hearty soup is a popular Cuban specialty. For a show-stopping presentation, top with a dollop of sour cream or crème fraîche, chopped red onions, cilantro, or hard-boiled egg, grated cheddar cheese, or thinly sliced lemons. For more heat, add some chopped jalapeños. For a meaty soup, cook a ham hock with the beans and shred the meat into the soup right before serving.

Cooking Time: Over 60 minutes
Serves: 4

1. In a large stock pot over medium heat, add the oil. Sauté the onions, carrots, celery, and garlic until softened, 5 to 8 minutes, stirring frequently.
2. Add the black beans, broth, and cumin and stir to combine. Bring to a boil.
3. Reduce the heat, cover, and simmer for 1½ to 2 hours, or until the beans are tender, stirring occasionally.
4. For a thicker soup, purée 3 cups of soup in a food processor and add back into the pot, or use an immersion blender to purée the beans directly in the pot.

7
SALADS

Just as vegetarian dishes have profited by the demand for more flavorful and nutritious produce, salads have reaped similar benefits. No longer simply a side dish, salads have become as inventive as the main course—in many instances, they have replaced the main course!

Be creative when making your salad. Go for flavor, color, and texture. Look beyond the standard iceberg-and-tomato combination. With so many lettuces providing superior and distinctive flavors and offering different degrees of crunch, it is easy to build a salad that has great balance and interest. Use a variety of greens and combine them with a huge spectrum of accompaniments, including vegetables in season, fresh or dried fruits, creamy or sharp cheeses, and crunchy nuts, seeds, or croutons.

With more flavorful ingredients starring in the salad bowl, go for light and simple dressings, sparingly applied. Heavy, leaden toppings that overwhelm delicate leaves and vibrant flavors are a thing of the past. Now, simple vinaigrettes share the limelight.

So use your imagination, and have fun. A salad is whatever you want it to be.

Salad Tips:

- Explore your local farmers' markets. They offer a wide variety of freshly picked, locally grown vegetables and fruits at reasonable prices. Better yet, plant your own vegetable or herb garden, so delicious salad fixings are no further than your back yard!
- Experiment with different lettuces: peppery arugula and watercress; soft lettuces (also known as butterhead), including the Boston and Bibb varieties; and crisp and slightly bitter endive, escarole, and radicchio are now widely available and add character to your salads. For crunch, use ro-

maine, green or red leaf, oak leaf, or cabbage. I like to use a combination of lettuces for added flavor, texture, and presentation value. You can choose whichever varieties appeal to you and look best at the market.

- Now most supermarkets offer premixed salad varieties, usually labeled gourmet salad mix or *mesclun,* a French word for mixture, either in a self-serve bin or packaged.
- Look for vibrant green leaves for greater vitamin A content.
- Choose greens with crisp leaves. Avoid any that are slimy, wilted, or have an odor.
- Salad greens are perishable. Store greens and vegetables in the refrigerator, and try to use them within three to five days for optimum freshness. Generally, thicker leaves and tighter heads last the longest. For better storage, keep greens in an airtight plastic bag or container.
- Store tomatoes at room temperature to preserve flavor.
- Thoroughly wash lettuce, vegetables, and fruits just before using them. Dirt, bugs, and worms are some of the little nuisances that find their way into fresh produce. Even if you buy "prewashed" packaged veggie or lettuce mixes, it is recommended that you rinse them first.
- To revive wilted greens, soak then in icy water for five minutes.
- Use a salad spinner to remove excess water after washing. This machine efficiently dries greens, keeping them crisp longer. Make sure not to overcrowd the spinner, or it will not be able to properly do its job.
- For easiest eating, tear or cut lettuce and cut vegetables into 1- to 1½ -inch pieces.
- Fresh fruit, dried fruit, cheeses, or toasted nuts or seeds add protein and texture to salads. Experiment with a grapefruit, avocado, and baby lettuce mix, or a combination of pear, walnut, and crumbled blue cheese on arugula.
- Add leftover beans, pasta, chicken, or fish to make your salad a meal in itself. Other great add-ins are olives, arti-

choke hearts, hearts of palm, and croutons. Croutons add extra crunch to your salad. Find your favorite packaged variety, or use leftover bread to make your own. To make croutons, melt 2 tablespoons of butter, add 2 cloves of crushed garlic, and let the mixture sit for 10 minutes. Cut 4 large pieces of French or Italian white bread into 1-inch cubes and toss them with the garlic butter. Spread the bread cubes on a cookie sheet and bake them in a preheated 350-degree oven for 10 to 15 minutes, or until they are golden brown. Let the croutons cool before serving.

- Use a variety of cooked, grilled, or fresh vegetables and fresh herbs in your salad. Mix in fennel, radishes, jicama, steamed haricots verts, or snow peas for added crunch. Lemony chervil, chives, dill, and basil all add interesting flavor.

- There are now many packaged salad and vegetables mixes. Use them for convenience. In a pinch, use fixings from the supermarket salad bar.

- As a general guide, figure about 2 cups of loosely packed greens per person for a side salad, less if there are a lot of vegetables or other additions. Eight loosely packed cups of greens equals about 4 to 7 ounces (depending on the type of lettuce you choose). You'll need about one half cup of salad dressing to coat a salad for four. It is not necessary to use all the dressing the recipe calls for.

- Fixing a salad does not need to be a precise effort. Unlike baking or cooking, it is not essential to use exact measurements. Choose vegetables you enjoy. If you love tomatoes or onions, put in as many as you want! Feel free to exchange onions for scallions or chives. Use cherry, Roma, or beefsteak tomatoes instead of salad tomatoes when they look good.

- Don't overload your salad with heavy dressings. Less dressing saves calories and lets you taste what you are eating.

Make your own dressings and use them sparingly, just enough to coat the salad lightly. Sample different varieties of high quality extra-virgin olive oils and premium vinegars to see which you like best. For a change of pace, experiment with a variety of flavored oils and vinegars. Try lemon, herb, or garlic oils or cider, balsamic, red wine, raspberry, or champagne vinegar; or add your favorite fresh herbs to your dressing for a light and lively flavor. Other dressing intensifiers are mustard (prepared or dried), honey, Worcestershire sauce, poppy seeds, garlic, and dried herbs.

• When making a salad in advance, or if you're bringing it to a party, wait to dress the salad until just before serving.

Chunky Salad

Dressing:

½ cup extra-virgin olive oil
¼ cup balsamic vinegar
1 teaspoon sugar
½ teaspoon salt

Salad:

10 radishes, halved or
  quartered if large
10 mushrooms, halved or
  quartered if large
1 large carrot, cut into 1-inch
  pieces
1 medium red bell pepper,
  seeded and cut into 1-
  inch pieces
1 medium yellow or orange
  bell pepper, seeded and
  cut into 1-inch pieces
1 large celery stalk, cut into
  1-inch pieces
1 medium cucumber, seeded,
  halved, and cut into
  1-inch pieces
1 cup blanched haricot verts
1 cup red or yellow cherry or
  pear tomatoes, halved
  if large

This colorful salad features chunks of raw or quickly blanched vegetables that stand on their own. Cut the vegetables into large pieces so their flavors shine through. The vegetables are the stars of this salad, so just a light oil and vinegar dressing is recommended.

1. Prepare the dressing: In a clean jar, add the oil, vinegar, sugar, and salt and shake well to combine. (You can also mix the dressing in a bowl using a wire whisk). Set aside.
2. Prepare the salad: In a large bowl, combine the radishes, mushrooms, carrots, red peppers, yellow peppers, celery, cucumbers, haricot verts, tomatoes, and enough dressing to coat the vegetables. Toss to combine.

Antipasto

This colorful Italian-inspired salad combines vibrant vegetables with flavorful meats and cheeses. You can toss it with chopped lettuce, or decoratively arrange the toppings on large lettuce leaves. Make sure to seek out full-flavored meats and cheese for optimal enjoyment. This salad is a great way to add protein to an otherwise vegetarian meal and to use up odds and ends in your refrigerator. Make your own Italian herb dressing or use a robust bottled Italian dressing.

1. Prepare the dressing: In a clean jar, add the oil, vinegar, oregano, pepper, and salt and shake well to combine. (You can also mix the dressing in a bowl using a wire whisk). Set aside.

2. Prepare the salad: In a large bowl or on a large platter, combine the lettuce, tomatoes, artichoke hearts, olives, chickpeas, roasted peppers, pepperoncinis, onions, salami, prosciutto, Fontina, and enough dressing to coat the salad. Toss to combine.

Dressing:

½ cup extra-virgin olive oil
¼ cup red wine vinegar
1 teaspoon oregano
½ teaspoon black pepper
¼ teaspoon salt

Salad:

8 cups loosely packed, green or red leaf lettuce
2 large ripe tomatoes, cut into wedges
1 cup drained marinated artichoke hearts
1 cup black Italian olives
1 cup rinsed and drained canned chickpeas
1 cup roasted red peppers or fresh red peppers (optional)
1 cup pepperoncini (optional)
½ cup sliced red onion
¼ pound Genoa salami, thinly sliced
¼ pound prosciutto, cappicola, sopressata, or pepperoni, thinly sliced
¼ pound Fontina, provolone, or Asiago cheese, thinly sliced

Fresh Tomato, Basil, and Mozzarella Salad

Salad:

4 large ripe tomatoes, sliced
½ pound fresh mozzarella
   cheese, drained and
   thinly sliced
⅓ cup chopped or torn fresh
   basil

Dressing:

2 to 3 tablespoons extra-virgin
   olive oil
1 teaspoon kosher or sea salt
½ teaspoon freshly ground
   black pepper

This tri-colored salad salutes the colors, flag, and tastes of Italy. It is best made in the height of summer, when in-season tomatoes are bursting with color and flavor and fresh basil is abundant. Fresh mozzarella, formerly only sold in specialty stores, is now found in most large supermarkets. It is packaged with liquid to maintain its moisture and has a distinctively light flavor and texture. Let the flavor of the vegetables and herbs shine through with just a light drizzle of high-quality olive oil, kosher or sea salt, and freshly ground black pepper.

1. Prepare the salad: On a platter, alternate slices of tomato and mozzarella slices to form 3 rows. Sprinkle with the basil.
2. Lightly drizzle the salad with the oil and sprinkle with salt and pepper.

Spinach, Bacon, and Mushroom Salad

This classic salad tops a mound of nutritious spinach with hard-boiled eggs, thinly sliced mushrooms, red onion, and crunchy bacon for a delightful combination of tastes and textures. I like to top this salad with a sweet and spicy honey-mustard dressing, but you can use a simple vinaigrette or a creamy ranch dressing. Whether you choose bagged spinach or bundled spinach, look for tender, small leaves and be sure to rinse them well, as grit clings tightly to these precious greens. For a nice change, substitute cooked pancetta for the bacon or add a sprinkling of goat, Gruyère, or blue cheese.

Dressing:

½ cup extra-virgin olive oil
2 tablespoons cider or red
  wine vinegar
2 tablespoons honey-mustard
1 teaspoon sugar or honey
½ teaspoon salt

Salad:

8 cups loosely packed, spinach
  leaves, stems removed
3 hard-boiled eggs, peeled and
  thinly sliced
2 cups sliced mushrooms
⅓ cup thinly sliced red onions
½ pound bacon, crisply
  cooked and crumbled

1. Prepare the dressing: In a clean jar, add the oil, vinegar, honey-mustard, sugar, and salt and shake well to combine. (You can also mix the dressing in a bowl using a wire whisk). Set aside.
2. Prepare the salad: Place the spinach in a large bowl. Top with the eggs, mushrooms, onions, bacon, and enough dressing to coat the salad. Toss to combine.

Coleslaw

Dressing:

1 large clove garlic

2 tablespoons chopped red onions

½ cup Hidden Valley buttermilk ranch dressing or other ranch dressing

Salad:

1 16-ounce package shredded coleslaw mix or shredded cabbage

2 tablespoons caraway seeds

Coleslaw is a refreshing change from a green salad and is a nice addition to sausage and peppers, fish tacos, or any grilled entrée. This coleslaw is seasoned with a zesty garlic-buttermilk ranch dressing and then sprinkled with caraway seeds. Shred or slice a fifty-fifty mixture of green and red cabbage in your food processor and toss with some shredded carrots for a more colorful version. For tremendous time savings, look for a packaged shredded cabbage and carrot mix in your market's produce section. One note: Coleslaw will give off a lot of moisture and shrink considerably. If you are making the salad ahead, dress it sparingly and add more just before serving, if necessary.

1. Prepare the dressing: In a food processor fitted with a metal chopping blade, with the motor running, add the garlic and purée. Add the onions and ranch dressing and pulse until combined. Set aside.
2. Prepare the salad: In a large bowl, combine the shredded cabbage and enough dressing to coat the salad. Toss to combine. Top with the caraway seeds.

Tomato Salsa

Chunky, homestyle salsa, also known as salsa fresca, is a mainstay of Mexican-American dining. It features a simple but winning combination of fresh and juicy chopped ripe tomatoes, jalapeño pepper, garlic, cilantro, and onion. It's perfect with the Chile Relleno Phyllo Bake, burritos, tacos, quesadillas, or just with tortilla chips. A word of caution: Make the salsa just before you need it. If you make it too far ahead, it will become watery and will lose some of its distinct flavors.

2 to 3 large ripe tomatoes, seeded and coarsely chopped
¼ cup chopped red onions
¼ cup chopped fresh cilantro
1 tablespoon fresh lime or lemon juice (optional)
1 teaspoon finely chopped fresh jalapeño peppers
1 teaspoon minced garlic (optional)
½ teaspoon salt
1 to 2 dashes Tabasco, or other hot red pepper sauce (optional)

1. In a large bowl, add the tomatoes, onions, cilantro, lime juice, jalapeños, garlic, salt, and Tabasco and toss to combine.

Caesar Salad

Dressing:

1 clove garlic
½ cup extra-virgin olive oil
¼ cup mayonnaise
2 tablespoons freshly
    squeezed lemon juice
2 teaspoons Dijon mustard
1 teaspoon Worcestershire
    sauce
1 teaspoon anchovy paste,
    or chopped anchovies,
    or salt
1 teaspoon ground black
    pepper

Salad:

8 cups loosely packed romaine
    lettuce
½ cup shaved or grated
    Parmesan cheese
1 cup croutons
4 anchovy fillets (optional)

This classic salad, made with a creamy garlic dressing, is great with more than just Italian entrées. It adds a special touch to any meal it is served with, and becomes a meal in itself in the Chicken Caesar Wrap or Shrimp Caesar Wrap.

1. Prepare the dressing: In a food processor fitted with a metal chopping blade, with the motor running, add the garlic and purée. Add the oil, mayonnaise, lemon juice, mustard, Worcestershire sauce, anchovy paste, and pepper and process to combine. (You can also mix the dressing in a bowl using a wire whisk). Set aside.

2. Prepare the salad: In a large bowl, combine the lettuce and enough dressing to coat the lettuce. Add the cheese, croutons, and anchovies and toss again.

Greek Salad

This wonderful salad is loaded with crunchy cukes, red onions, tomatoes, kalamata olives, and feta cheese and is topped with an herbed-red wine vinaigrette. Try different kinds of feta cheese to find the one you like best. They vary in saltiness, and some are creamier than others. French feta is particularly good.

Dressing:

½ cup extra-virgin olive oil
¼ cup red wine vinegar
1 teaspoon Italian seasoning
1 teaspoon sugar

Salad:

5 cups loosely packed, chopped green or red leaf lettuce
1 cup seeded, chopped cucumbers
1 large ripe tomato, chopped
1 cup kalamata or Greek olives
¼ cup sliced red onions
¼ pound feta cheese, crumbled

1. Prepare the dressing: In a clean jar, add the oil, vinegar, Italian seasoning, and sugar and shake well to combine. (You can also mix the dressing in a bowl using a wire whisk). Set aside.
2. Prepare the salad: In a large bowl, combine the lettuce, cucumbers, tomatoes, olives, onions, feta cheese, and enough dressing to coat the salad. Toss to combine.

Mediterranean Salad

This delectable combination pairs sweetened dried cranberries, creamy goat cheese, and toasted, buttery pignoli (also known as pine nuts) with a variety of mixed greens and a light vinaigrette. The combination of tastes, color, and texture will make this salad a favorite for everyday and entertaining. Look for packaged salad mixes that include a variety of baby lettuces, or mix your own using different greens, including arugula and raddicchio, for a more flavorful and colorful salad.

Dressing:

½ cup extra-virgin olive oil
¼ cup balsamic vinegar
1 tablespoon Dijon mustard
1 teaspoon sugar
½ teaspoon salt

Salad:

8 cups loosely packed, mesculan or other lettuce mix
1 cup seeded and chopped cucumbers
1 cup dried cranberries
2 tablespoons finely chopped chives (optional)
½ cup pine nuts, lightly toasted
¼ pound goat cheese, crumbled

1. Prepare the dressing: In a clean jar, add the oil, vinegar, mustard, sugar, and salt and shake well to combine. (You can also mix the dressing in a bowl using a wire whisk). Set aside.
2. Prepare the salad: In a large bowl, combine the lettuce, cucumbers, cranberries, chives, and enough dressing to coat the salad. Toss to combine. Top with the pine nuts and goat cheese.

Pear, Walnut, Blue Cheese, and Arugula Salad

This unusual salad combines the sweetness of fall's ripe and succulent pears with the crunch of toasted walnuts and the piquancy of blue cheese. Use any lettuce you enjoy to balance the delightfully peppery arugula. For a special touch, make or buy spiced walnuts or pecans. This is a great salad for Thanksgiving or any autumnal dinner.

1. Prepare the dressing: In a clean jar, add the oil, vinegar, mustard, sugar, and salt and shake well to combine. (You can also mix the dressing in a bowl using a wire whisk). Set aside.

2. Prepare the salad: In a large bowl, combine the lettuce, arugula, onions, pears, and enough dressing to coat the salad. Toss to combine. Top with the walnuts and blue cheese.

Dressing:

½ cup extra-virgin olive or walnut oil
¼ cup balsamic vinegar
1 tablespoon Dijon mustard
1 teaspoon sugar
½ teaspoon salt

Salad:

5 cups loosely packed lettuce
3 cups loosely packed arugula
¼ cup thinly sliced red onions
3 ripe pears, peeled, cored, and sliced
1 cup chopped walnuts or pecans, lightly toasted
¼ pound blue cheese, crumbled

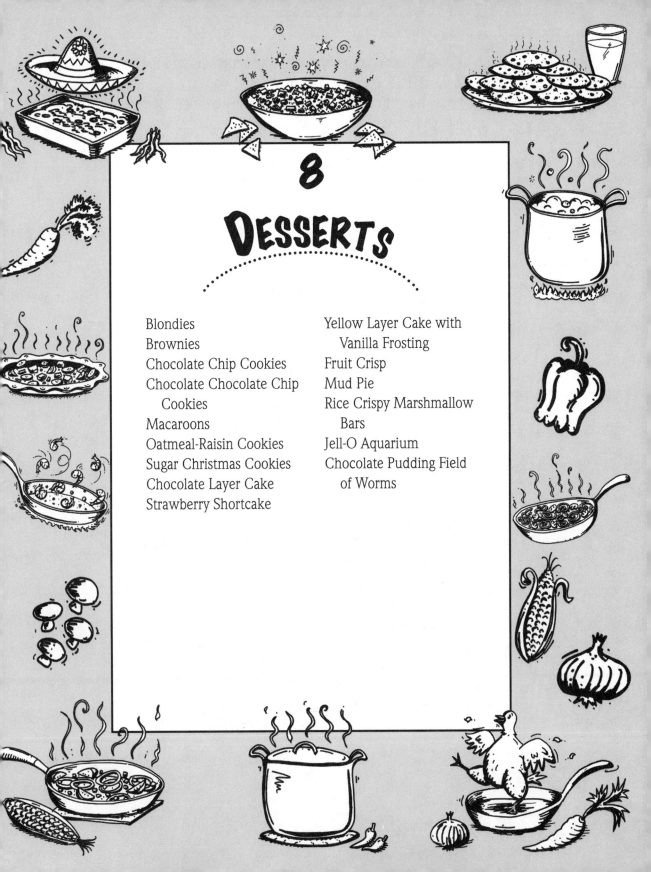

8

DESSERTS

Blondies
Brownies
Chocolate Chip Cookies
Chocolate Chocolate Chip
  Cookies
Macaroons
Oatmeal-Raisin Cookies
Sugar Christmas Cookies
Chocolate Layer Cake
Strawberry Shortcake

Yellow Layer Cake with
  Vanilla Frosting
Fruit Crisp
Mud Pie
Rice Crispy Marshmallow
  Bars
Jell-O Aquarium
Chocolate Pudding Field
  of Worms

I find the desserts my family enjoys the most are the same treats I looked forward to when I was a girl: cookies, brownies, fruit crisps, Jell-O and pudding creations, ice cream pie, and most special of all, birthday layer cakes! These treasures, which bring so much joy, actually require very little effort and time. Most take less than fifteen minutes to prepare and require half an hour or less to bake. Best of all, when it comes time to make dessert, there is no shortage of assistants. With little helpers willing to do tasting and mixing, it's as much an activity as an event.

Cookie Tips:

- Always preheat the oven for at least fifteen minutes before baking.
- Most cookie dough can be easily mixed in a large bowl with a sturdy spoon or your hands. When using an electric mixer or food processor, periodically scrape down the sides and bottom of the bowl for more even blending.
- Baking cookies on baking sheets lined with parchment paper prevents burned bottoms, stops the dough from spreading, and keeps baking sheets from getting dirty. Parchment paper (available at most kitchen supply stores) can be wiped down and reused.
- To prevent excess spreading, refrigerate cookie dough for half an hour before baking.
- After baking, place cookies on a cooling rack to prevent burned cookie bottoms.
- When baking bar cookies, line the baking pan with aluminum foil for easier cleanup. To easily line baking pans, turn the pan upside down and mold a sheet of foil over the outside of the pan, then flip the pan over and drop the foil inside. If the recipe calls for a greased pan, lightly spray or grease the foil. After cooling, gently lift out the foil with the bar cookies.

- Check cookies a couple of minutes before the minimum baking time. It is better to underbake cookies and brownies than to overbake them. Cookies will continue to bake when they are removed from the oven and will harden as they cool.

Cake Tips:

- Always preheat the oven for at least fifteen minutes before baking.
- For optimal results, use ingredients at room temperature, unless directed otherwise. Leave refrigerated items out for one to two hours to achieve the proper temperature.
- An electric mixer does an excellent job of creaming butter and sugar together and aerating the batter. The air incorporated into the batter gives the cake its light and fine-grained texture.
- Although thorough beating is important when creaming butter, sugar, and eggs, mix the dry ingredients just until they combine with the batter. Overmixing dry ingredients will undo much of the aeration achieved through creaming.
- Layer cake pans should be between one-half and two-thirds full. Use any excess batter for cupcakes.
- Don't try to "save time" by increasing the oven temperature for faster results. You'll end up with an overcooked outside and an undercooked inside.
- A cake is done when the top looks dry, a toothpick inserted into the center comes out with no crumbs clinging, and the cake springs back (leaving no depression) when lightly touched in the center. If the cake has started to shrink away from the sides of the pan, it is done. If the other signs are present, do not wait for this or the cake could be slightly dry.
- To remove a cake from its pan, run a sharp knife or frosting spatula around the sides of the pans to prevent sticking.

Then cover the pan with an inverted cooling rack (or your hand) and flip it over. The cake should drop out. To re-invert the cake, so it is right side up, cover it again with a cooling rack (or your hand) and repeat the process. Let the cake finish cooling on the rack.

- Cool cakes completely before frosting them. Freezing a cake for an hour before adding frosting will make it more stable and reduces its crumbs.

Blondies

This bar version of chocolate chip cookies is also known as butterscotch brownies. Because the dough cooks in a pan, it frees you from having to check the oven as frequently as when making trays of individual cookies. For a little change, add 1 cup of chopped walnuts to the batter, or try using a combination of chocolate chips and butterscotch chips.

2½ cups all-purpose flour
2 teaspoons baking powder
½ teaspoon salt
1 cup (2 sticks) butter, melted
1½ cups firmly packed brown sugar
2 teaspoons vanilla extract
3 eggs
2 cups semisweet chocolate chips

Baking Time: 25 to 30 minutes
Makes: Approximately 36 blondies

1. Preheat the oven to 350 degrees. Lightly grease a 13 × 9 × 2-inch baking pan.
2. In a medium bowl, mix the flour, baking powder, and salt. Set aside.
3. In a large bowl, using a sturdy spoon or an electric mixer, combine the butter, brown sugar, and vanilla.
4. Add the eggs and beat until thoroughly combined.
5. Gradually add the dry ingredients and mix well.
6. Stir in the chocolate chips.
7. Pour the batter into the prepared pan. Smooth the top with a spatula.
8. Bake for 25 to 30 minutes, or until golden and a toothpick inserted in the center comes out almost clean. The blondies should still be slightly moist in the center, but should bounce back when touched.
9. Cool completely on a cooling rack before cutting.

Brownies

1¼ cups all-purpose flour
½ teaspoon baking powder
¼ teaspoon salt
1 cup (2 sticks) butter, melted
2 cups granulated sugar
1 tablespoon vanilla extract
3 eggs
¾ cup unsweetened cocoa
1½ cups semisweet chocolate
   chips

A dense, rich, fudgy brownie is always pretty hard to resist, but this super-chocolatey version is impossible to say no to. They are a snap to make, and any extras store beautifully in the freezer (just waiting to be transformed into brownie à la mode). For an attractive presentation, mix white chocolate chips or chunks with the semisweet chips; or, if you are a nut lover, add 1 cup of walnuts or pecans to the batter and sprinkle another ½ cup on top. The secret for sensational brownies is to slightly underbake them. This gives them their thick, lush texture. If you prefer a more cake-like brownie, bake for an additional 3 to 5 minutes, or until a toothpick inserted in the center comes out dry.

Baking Time: 30 to 35 minutes
Makes: Approximately 36 brownies

1. Preheat the oven to 350 degrees. Lightly grease a 13 × 9 × 2-inch baking pan.
2. In a medium bowl, mix the flour, baking powder, and salt. Set aside.
3. In a large bowl, using a sturdy spoon or an electric mixer, combine the butter, sugar, and vanilla.

4. Add the eggs and beat until well blended.
5. Add the cocoa and beat until thoroughly combined.
6. Gradually add the dry ingredients and mix well.
7. Stir in 1 cup of the chocolate chips.
8. Pour the batter into the prepared pan. Smooth the top with a spatula. Sprinkle the remaining ½ cup of chips on top.
9. Bake for 30 to 35 minutes, or until a toothpick inserted in the center comes out almost clean. The brownies should still be slightly moist in the center, but should bounce back when touched.
10. Cool completely on a cooling rack before cutting.

Chocolate Chip Cookies

2¼ cups all-purpose flour
1 teaspoon baking soda
½ teaspoon salt
1 cup (2 sticks) butter,
    softened
¾ cup granulated sugar
¾ cup firmly packed brown
    sugar
1 teaspoon vanilla extract
2 eggs
2 cups semisweet chocolate
    chips or chocolate
    chunks
1 cup chopped walnuts
    (optional)

This true classic will never go out of style. Today it has been updated to "monster-size"—cookies 4 or 5 inches in diameter, at least two or three times what was originally called for. For giant cookies, use a ¼-cup measure, place the cookies at least 4 inches apart, and add approximately 3 minutes to the baking time. For "gourmet" looking (and tasting) cookies, substitute 12 ounces of chopped chocolate from a high-quality semisweet or bittersweet chocolate bar for the chips.

Baking Time: 8 to 12 minutes
Makes: Approximately 48 2-inch cookies

1. Preheat the oven to 375 degrees.
2. In a medium bowl, mix the flour, baking soda, and salt. Set aside.
3. In a large bowl, using a sturdy spoon or an electric mixer, cream the butter until fluffy and lightened in color.
4. Add the white and brown sugars and beat until well blended.

5. Add the vanilla and eggs. Beat until thoroughly combined.
6. Gradually add the dry ingredients and mix well.
7. Stir in the chocolate chips and walnuts.
8. Drop the dough by rounded tablespoons 2 inches apart onto ungreased baking sheets.
9. Bake for 8 to 12 minutes, or until the cookies are golden and the edges are lightly browned.
10. Let stand for 1 minute. Remove the cookies from the baking sheets to a cooling rack.

Chocolate Chocolate Chip Cookies

2¼ cups all-purpose flour
1 teaspoon baking soda
½ teaspoon salt
¾ cup unsweetened cocoa
1 cup (2 sticks) butter,
    softened
¾ cup granulated sugar
¾ cup firmly packed brown
    sugar
2 teaspoons vanilla extract
2 eggs
2 cups semisweet chocolate
    chips or chocolate
    chunks

For true chocoholics, these cookies offer a double dose of delight—chocolate cookie dough and chocolate chips. A word of caution: Their darker color makes it harder to judge readiness. Be sure to start checking the cookies before the minimum cooking time and watch for burning edges and bottoms. Use insulated baking sheets, or double-stack two sheets to prevent overbaking. To add a little character, I like to combine white chocolate chips or chunks with semisweet chips.

Baking Time: 7 to 12 minutes
Makes: Approximately 48 cookies

1. Preheat the oven to 350 degrees.
2. In a medium bowl, mix the flour, baking soda, salt, and cocoa. Set aside.
3. In a large bowl, using a sturdy spoon or an electric mixer, cream the butter until fluffy and lightened in color.
4. Add the white and brown sugars and beat until well blended.
5. Add the vanilla and eggs. Beat until thoroughly combined.
6. Gradually add the dry ingredients and mix well.
7. Stir in the chocolate chips.

8. Drop the dough by rounded tablespoons 2 inches apart onto ungreased baking sheets.
9. Bake for 7 to 12 minutes, or until set, being careful not to burn. The centers will feel slightly firm to the touch.
10. Let stand for 1 minute. Remove the cookies from the baking sheets to a cooling rack.

Macaroons

⅓ cup all-purpose flour
2¾ cups shredded sweetened coconut (approximately 8 ounces)
⅛ teaspoon salt
⅔ cup sweetened condensed milk (not evaporated milk) (approximately 7 ounces)
1 teaspoon vanilla extract

I have been making these cookies with my son since he was two years old. Needing only five ingredients and no fancy mixing, they are easy enough for him to prepare. But be careful—they are so delicious, they are dangerously easy to eat. Two tips for foolproof baking: Because macaroon dough tends to be a little sticky, line the baking sheets with parchment paper or greased aluminum foil for easier cleanup. Also, the cookie bottoms have a tendency to bake quickly. Use insulated baking sheets or double-stack baking sheets for better protection, and check the macaroon bottoms during baking. For a special treat, I like to dip my macaroon bottoms into melted dark chocolate after baking.

Baking Time: 13 to 18 minutes
Makes: Approximately 12 macaroons

1. Preheat the oven to 350 degrees. Grease a baking sheet well.
2. In a large bowl, mix the flour, coconut, and salt.
3. Add the condensed milk and vanilla and stir well. The batter will be thick and sticky.
4. Roll the dough into 2-inch balls or drop generous tablespoons onto the baking sheet about 2 inches apart. Bake for 13 to 18 minutes, or until the macaroons are golden and firm to the touch.
5. Remove the cookies from the baking sheet immediately to prevent sticking, and cool on a cooling rack.

Desserts

Oatmeal-Raisin Cookies

Here's another childhood favorite. These aromatic, chewy classics are wonderful on their own, with a large glass of cold milk, or with a steaming cup of hot tea. Use either quick-cooking or old-fashioned oats. Old-fashioned oats make chewier cookies; quick-cooking oats absorb moisture faster and tend to make crisper cookies. Do not use instant oatmeal.

1½ cups all-purpose flour
1 teaspoon baking soda
½ teaspoon salt
1 teaspoon ground cinnamon
½ teaspoon ground nutmeg
   (optional)
1 cup (2 sticks) butter,
   softened
1 cup firmly packed brown
   sugar
½ cup granulated sugar
1 teaspoon vanilla extract
2 eggs
3 cups uncooked oatmeal
1½ cups raisins

Baking Time: 8 to 12 minutes
Makes: Approximately 30 cookies

1. Preheat the oven to 375 degrees.
2. In a medium bowl, mix the flour, baking soda, salt, cinnamon, and nutmeg. Set aside.
3. In a large bowl, using a sturdy spoon or an electric mixer, cream the butter until fluffy and lightened in color.
4. Add both sugars and beat until well blended.
5. Add the vanilla and eggs. Beat until thoroughly combined.
6. Gradually add the dry ingredients and mix well.
7. Gradually add the oatmeal and raisins until combined.
8. Drop the dough by rounded tablespoons 2 inches apart onto ungreased baking sheets.
9. Bake for 8 to 12 minutes, or until the cookies are golden and the edges are lightly browned.
10. Let stand for 1 minute. Remove the cookies from the baking sheets to a cooling rack.

Sugar Christmas Cookies

Cookies:

2½ cups all-purpose flour
¼ teaspoon salt
1 teaspoon baking powder
1 cup (2 sticks) butter,
    softened
1 cup granulated sugar
2 teaspoons vanilla extract
1 egg
Colored sugar, sprinkles, or
    candies (optional)

Icing:

3 cups confectioners' sugar
2 to 3 tablespoons milk

Whether it's a holiday or not, it seems I am always making rolled sugar cookies for one school event or another. My son Alex loves picking out different cutters and then decorating the cookies, especially when candy is involved! While many people have a fear of rolling out cookie dough, once you get the hang of it, it's as easy as can be. Just make sure to follow these three rules and you'll have perfect cookies every time: First, refrigerate the dough until it is no longer sticky but is not so cold that it will crack during rolling. Second, use a light sprinkling of flour when rolling out the dough to prevent sticking. Third, don't roll the cookies too thinly, or they'll be difficult to handle.

Baking Time: 8 to 13 minutes
Makes: Approximately 48 cookies

1. Prepare the cookies: In a medium bowl, mix the flour, salt, and baking powder. Set aside.
2. In a large bowl, using a sturdy spoon or an electric mixer, cream the butter until fluffy and lightened in color.
3. Add the sugar and beat until well blended.
4. Add the vanilla and egg. Beat until thoroughly combined.
5. Gradually add the dry ingredients and mix well.
6. Scrape the dough onto a sheet of plastic wrap. It will be soft and sticky. Press the dough together to form a flat disc between ¼- and ½-inch thick. Wrap tightly

and refrigerate until firm, 1 to 2 hours (or freeze for 30 to 40 minutes).

7. When the cookies are ready to roll out, preheat the oven to 350 degrees. Take out the baking sheets.

8. On a lightly floured surface, with a lightly floured rolling pin, roll out the dough ⅛- to ¼-inch thick, lifting and turning the dough frequently to prevent sticking (add additional flour if necessary to prevent sticking). With flour-dipped cookie cutters or a sharp knife, cut the dough into desired shapes. Carefully transfer the shapes to ungreased baking sheets.

9. Decorate the cookies with colored sugars, sprinkles, or candies. If decorating cookies with icing, bake before frosting.

10. Bake for 8 to 13 minutes, or until the cookies are firm to the touch and the edges are golden.

11. Let the cookies stand for 1 minute. Remove the cookies from the baking sheets to a cooling rack. Cool completely before frosting.

12. Prepare the icing: Combine the confectioners' sugar with 2 tablespoons of milk. Mix until smooth and creamy, but stiff enough that the frosting does not flow from a spoon. If necessary, add additional milk or sugar, ½ teaspoon at a time, to reach the desired consistency. For a lighter glaze, add additional milk, ½ teaspoon at a time, until the mixture flows from a spoon. Spread the icing or glaze with a small spatula or brush. Top with sugar or candy decorations before the glaze dries. If you want to pipe icing on top of a glaze, wait for the glaze to dry first. Allow the decorated cookies to dry completely before storing (about 2 hours).

Chocolate Layer Cake

Cake:

2 cups all-purpose flour
1 teaspoon baking soda
½ teaspoon salt
¾ cup unsweetened cocoa
½ cup (1 stick) butter,
    softened
1½ cups granulated sugar
2 teaspoons vanilla extract
2 eggs
1¼ cups buttermilk

Frosting:

3¾ cups confectioners' sugar
    (1 pound)
½ cup unsweetened cocoa
½ cup (1 stick) butter,
    softened
1 teaspoon vanilla extract
⅓ cup milk (approximately)

This is the quintessential layer birthday cake. Rich and chocolatey, but not too sweet, with creamy chocolate frosting. It also makes great cupcakes for school and work parties. For foolproof decorating, the frosting should be soft, pliant, and smooth enough to spread without tearing the cake.

Baking Time: 25 to 35 minutes
Serves: 12 to 14

1. Prepare the cake: Preheat the oven to 350 degrees. Lightly grease and flour two 9-inch cake pans.
2. In a medium bowl, mix the flour, baking soda, salt, and cocoa. Set aside.
3. In a large bowl, cream the butter, sugar, and vanilla with an electric mixer on medium speed until light and fluffy, about 2 minutes, stopping twice to scrape the bowl and beater(s) with a spatula.
4. Add the eggs, one at a time, beating well after each addition.
5. On low speed, alternate adding one-third of the dry ingredients with half of the buttermilk, mixing for 5 to 10 seconds after each addition. Do not blend each addition in fully before adding the next. When everything has been added, scrape the bowl and beater(s) and mix until blended and smooth (about 5 seconds). Do not overmix.
6. Divide the batter evenly between the prepared pans, and smooth the tops with a spatula. Place the pans on

the middle rack of the oven, leaving 2 inches between the pans and the oven walls.

7. Bake for 25 to 35 minutes, or until a toothpick inserted in the center comes out clean and the cakes spring back when lightly touched. Do not wait for the cakes to pull away from the sides of the pans.

8. Cool the cakes in their pans on a cooling rack for 15 minutes. Loosen the sides with a thin knife and carefully remove the cake layers. Cool completely before frosting.

9. Prepare the frosting: Pour the confectioners' sugar (1 cup at a time) and cocoa into a sifter or wire strainer placed over a medium bowl. Mix until blended.

10. In a large bowl, cream the butter with an electric mixer on medium speed until light and fluffy, about 1 minute.

11. Gradually add half of the dry ingredients and beat well.

12. Add the vanilla and half of the milk. The mixture will be dry and crumbly. Add the rest of the dry ingredients and enough milk for the desired spreading consistency. Beat on high until smooth.

•••••••••••••••••••••••••••••

Variations:

Cupcakes: *Line muffin tins with paper or foil liners. (Liners keep cupcakes moist and make them easier to remove.) Fill tins half to two-thirds full. Bake at 350 degrees for 18 to 23 minutes, or until the tops are firm and a toothpick inserted into a cupcake comes out clean. Cool the cupcakes completely in the tins on a cooling rack. Remove and frost. Makes 24 cupcakes.*

Sheet Cake: *Batter can be baked in a 13 × 9 × 2-inch pan. Bake a sheet cake for 35 to 45 minutes.*

•••••••••••••••••••••••••••••

Strawberry Shortcake

Strawberries:

2 pints strawberries, cleaned,
    hulled, and sliced
⅓ cup granulated sugar
8 to 12 whole strawberries,
    for garnish (optional)

Shortcake:

2 cups all-purpose flour
¼ cup granulated sugar
1 tablespoon baking powder
½ teaspoon salt
½ cup (1 stick) butter, chilled
    and cut into large
    pieces
⅔ cup milk, plus extra for
    glazing
3 tablespoons butter, softened

Whipped cream:

2 cups heavy cream
3 tablespoons confectioners'
    sugar
1 teaspoon vanilla extract

These individual shortcakes are a snap to prepare. Simple biscuits are filled with seasonally sweet strawberries and the always-welcomed whipped cream. But don't limit yourself to just strawberries. Choose from the farmers' markets' finest: blueberries, peaches, and raspberries are all delicious!

Baking Time: 13 to 18 minutes
Serves: 8 to 10

1. Preheat the oven to 450 degrees. Take out a baking sheet.
2. Prepare the strawberries: In a medium bowl, mix the strawberries with the sugar. Set aside.
3. Prepare the shortcakes: In a food processor fitted with a metal chopping blade, add the flour, sugar, baking powder, and salt. Pulse to combine (about 4 pulses).
4. Add the butter and pulse until the mixture resembles coarse crumbs (about 10 pulses).
5. Add the milk and pulse until just combined and evenly moistened (about 4 or 5 pulses). Do not allow the dough to form a ball. (Shortcakes can also be made easily by hand. Combine the dry ingredients in a bowl. Add the butter and work the mixture with your fingertips until it resembles coarse crumbs. Add the milk and stir gently until just combined.)

6. Transfer the dough to a lightly floured surface. Knead, by pushing the dough with the palms of your hands, for about 30 seconds to make the dough less sticky.

7. Pat or gently roll the dough until it is ½-inch thick. Using lightly floured 3-inch round cookie cutters or a knife, cut out the biscuits (scraps can be pressed together for additional biscuits). Transfer the biscuits to an ungreased baking sheet and brush the tops with milk.

8. Bake for 13 to 18 minutes, or until golden and the tops are firm.

9. Cool the shortcakes on a cooling rack for 10 minutes. Split the cakes horizontally into 2 layers and spread the cut sides lightly with butter.

10. Just before serving, prepare the whipped cream: In a large bowl, with an electric mixer on medium-high speed, whip the cream to soft peaks. Add the sugar and vanilla and beat until stiff peaks form. Do not overbeat.

11. Place the bottoms of the shortcakes, cut side up, on a serving plate. Top with the strawberries and whipped cream. Place remaining shortcake on top, cut side down. Top with strawberries and whipped cream. Garnish with whole strawberries.

Yellow Layer Cake with Vanilla Frosting

Cake:

2½ cups cake flour
2 teaspoons baking powder
½ teaspoon salt
¾ cup (1½ sticks) butter, softened
1½ cups granulated sugar
1 teaspoon vanilla extract
3 eggs
1 cup milk

Frosting:

3¾ cups confectioners' sugar (1 pound)
½ cup (1 stick) butter, softened
2 teaspoons vanilla extract
¼ cup milk (approximately)

Celebrating has never been easier! This light and luscious butter cake is perfect for any holiday or event. Chocolate frosting is also good with the cake.

Baking Time: 25 to 35 minutes
Serves: 12 to 14

1. Prepare the cake: Preheat the oven to 350 degrees. Lightly grease and flour two 9-inch cake pans.
2. In a medium bowl, mix the cake flour, baking powder, and salt. Set aside.
3. In a large bowl, cream the butter, sugar, and vanilla with an electric mixer on medium speed until light and fluffy, about 2 minutes, stopping twice to scrape the bowl and beater(s) with a spatula.
4. Add the eggs, one at a time, beating well after each addition.
5. On low speed, alternate adding one-third of the dry ingredients with half of the milk, mixing for 5 to 10 seconds after each addition. Do not blend each addition in fully before adding the next. When everything has been added, scrape the bowl and beater(s), and mix until blended and smooth (about 5 seconds). Do not overmix.
6. Divide the batter evenly between the prepared pans and smooth the tops with a spatula. Place the pans on the middle rack of the oven, leaving 2 inches between the pans and the oven walls.

Desserts

7. Bake for 25 to 35 minutes, or until lightly golden, a toothpick inserted in the center comes out clean, and the cakes spring back when lightly touched. Do not wait for the cakes to pull away from the sides of the pans.

8. Cool the cakes in their pans on a cooling rack for 15 minutes. Loosen the sides with a thin knife and carefully remove the cake layers. Cool completely before frosting.

9. Prepare the frosting: Pour the confectioners' sugar (1 cup at a time) into a sifter or wire strainer placed over a medium bowl.

10. In a large bowl, cream the butter with an electric mixer on medium speed until light and fluffy, about 1 minute.

11. Gradually add half of the sugar and beat well.

12. Add the vanilla and half of the milk. The mixture will be dry and crumbly. Add the rest of the sugar and enough milk for the desired spreading consistency. Beat on high until smooth.

....

Variations:

Cupcakes: *Line muffin tins with paper or foil liners. (Liners keep cupcakes moist and make them easier to remove.) Fill tins half to two-thirds full. Bake at 350 degrees for 18 to 23 minutes, or until the tops are firm and a toothpick inserted into a cupcake comes out clean. Cool the cupcakes completely in the tins on a cooling rack. Remove and frost. Makes 24 cupcakes.*

Sheet Cake: *Batter can be baked in a 13 × 9 × 2-inch pan. Bake a sheet cake for 35 to 45 minutes.*

....

Fruit Crisp

Fruit Filling:

5 to 6 cups fruit or berries
2 tablespoons fresh lemon
    juice (optional)
2 tablespoons all-purpose flour
½ cup granulated sugar

Topping:

1 cup all-purpose flour
1 cup firmly packed brown
    sugar
½ cup uncooked oatmeal
    (optional)
2 teaspoons ground cinnamon
¼ teaspoon salt
½ cup (1 stick) butter, cut into
    pieces

This delicious fruit dessert is easy to assemble and is a wonderful way to end a meal all year round. For the best taste, choose fruit in season, at the peak of its flavor. In the fall and winter, use apples and pears. In the summer, try a combination of blueberries, strawberries, peaches, and cherries. For a more attractive presentation, bake and serve the crisp in a deep, decorative, ovenproof baking dish.

Baking Time: 35 to 45 minutes
Serves: 6 to 8

1. Preheat the oven to 375 degrees.
2. Prepare the fruit filling: In a 1½- to 2-quart baking dish, mix the fruit, lemon juice, flour, and sugar. Set aside.
3. Prepare the topping: In a food processor fitted with a metal chopping blade, add the flour, brown sugar, oats, cinnamon, and salt. Pulse to mix (about 4 pulses).

Desserts

4. Add the butter and pulse until the mixture is moistened but crumbly (about 5 to 10 pulses).
5. Sprinkle the topping over the fruit.
6. Bake for 35 to 45 minutes, or until the top is browned and crisp and the filling is bubbling. Check during the second half of baking to make sure the top is not over-browning and that the filling is not bubbling over. Shield the top with foil and/or slip a foil-covered baking sheet under the crisp if necessary.
7. Cool slightly on a cooling rack. Serve warm.

Mud Pie

Cookie Crust:

1½ cups cookie crumbs (approximately 30 chocolate wafers or 15 Oreos)
¼ cup (½ stick) butter, melted
2 tablespoons sugar

Hot Fudge Sauce:

½ cup heavy cream
2 tablespoons butter, cut in pieces
2 cups semisweet chocolate chips (12 ounces)
1 teaspoon vanilla extract

1 quart coffee ice cream (or other flavor)

Whipped Cream:

1 cup heavy cream
2 tablespoons confectioners' sugar
½ teaspoon vanilla extract

This sought-after summertime dessert layers creamy ice cream, gooey fudge, and wonderful whipped cream in a crunchy chocolate-cookie crust. It has everyone's favorite flavors together in each bite. Choose your family's special ice cream, or layer different flavors to please everyone. Allow time for the pie to properly chill.

Baking Time: 5 minutes
Serves: 6 to 8

1. Preheat the oven to 350 degrees.
2. Prepare the cookie crust: Combine the crumbs, butter, and sugar in a food processor or medium bowl. Blend until moistened and smooth. Press the crust evenly into the bottom of a 9-inch pie pan.
3. Bake the crust for 5 minutes. Cool completely on a cooling rack.
4. Prepare the hot fudge sauce: In a saucepan on low heat, warm the cream and butter until just simmering (little bubbles form around edges).
5. Add the chocolate chips and stir until dissolved.
6. Add the vanilla and stir until completely blended. Remove from the heat and cool the sauce completely.

7. Spoon ½ cup of fudge into the crust. Freeze the crust for 30 minutes.

8. Soften the ice cream to spreading consistency. Fill the crust with ice cream, mounding up the center.

9. Freeze the pie for 1 to 2 hours, or until firm.

10. Spread the remaining fudge over the top of the ice cream, covering it completely. Smooth the top. Freeze for 30 minutes, or until serving.

11. Just before serving, prepare the whipped cream: In a large bowl, with an electric mixer on medium-high speed, whip the cream to soft peaks. Add the sugar and vanilla and beat until stiff peaks form. Do not overbeat. Spread the whipped cream on top of the fudge or pipe it decoratively around the edges of the crust.

12. Let the pie soften for 10 minutes for easier slicing.

Rice Crispy Marshmallow Bars

3 tablespoons butter
10 ounces marshmallows
     (approximately 40)
6 cups puffed rice cereal

These chewy rice cereal–marshmallow bars need no baking, so they're perfect for a quickly needed dessert or lunch box snack. For easier cleanup, line your pan with aluminum foil, leaving a 1-inch overhang, before adding the cereal mixture. After cooling, lift the foil and crispy bars out of the pan and peel off the foil. Use fresh marshmallows for best flavor and texture.

Baking Time: None
Makes: Approximately 36 bars

1. Lightly grease a $13 \times 9 \times 2$-inch baking pan.
2. In a medium saucepan, over low heat melt the butter.
3. Add the marshmallows, coat with butter, and stir until melted and smooth. Remove from the heat. (To melt the butter and marshmallows in the microwave, cook them together on high for 2 minutes. Stir to combine and microwave 1 minute more. Stir until smooth.)
4. Add the rice cereal to the marshmallow mixture in 3 batches, stirring to coat it well after each addition.
5. Using a lightly greased spatula, transfer the mixture to the baking pan. Distribute the mixture evenly.
6. Cool the mixture completely in the pan before cutting.

Jell-O Aquarium

I found the idea for this recipe in a parents' magazine and fell in love with it. Gummy fish and worms are added to crystal blue Jell-O to form an edible ocean. If you have an empty goldfish bowl, serve the dessert in it for a truly unusual presentation. If not, use a deep, medium-sized, clear glass bowl for optimum visual impact.

1 6-ounce package Berry Blue Jell-O, or other blue gelatin dessert mix
2 cups boiling water
2 cups cold water
12–16 gummy fish, worms, or other edible aquatic life

Baking Time: None
Serves: 4

1. In a medium glass bowl, pour in the Jell-O mix. Add the boiling water and stir until completely dissolved, at least 2 minutes.
2. Stir in 2 cups cold water.
3. Refrigerate until the Jell-O just begins to set, about 1½ hours. It should still be in a liquid state, but thickening.
4. Using your fingers or a sharp knife, press the gummy fish into the Jell-O, at varying depths, so the fish are swimming at different levels, as if creating a fish tank. Refrigerate for 1½ to 2 hours, or until completely set.

Chocolate Pudding Field of Worms

16 Oreo cookies, or other
    chocolate sandwich
    cookies, crushed
1 5-ounce package Jell-O
    Cook & Serve choco-
    late pudding, or other
    pudding mix
3 cups milk
12 gummy worms

This unappetizing title doesn't give this dessert its due. This kid-friendly treat pairs chocolate pudding with crushed Oreo cookies to simulate a muddy field crawling with candy gummy worms. It's a gruesomely delicious and devastatingly easy dessert.

Baking Time: None
Serves: 4

1. In a 9 × 9-inch or 8 × 8-inch baking pan, layer half of the Oreos, reserving the rest.
2. In a medium saucepan over medium heat, dissolve the pudding mix into the milk.
3. Stir constantly until the mixture comes to a full boil. Remove from the heat.
4. Add the chocolate pudding to the Oreos, cover the surface with plastic wrap, and refrigerate for 1 hour, or until ready to serve.
5. Top with remaining Oreos. Arrange gummy worms as if they are crawling on top of and in the cookie "dirt."

Index

Recipes That Kids—and Dad—Will Love!

At the end of a busy workday, the next-to-the-last thing you want is to fix a time-consuming meal. And the *last* thing you want is to hear your kids complain about what you've cooked! With over 175 recipes, *Working Mom's Fast & Easy Kid-Friendly Meals* can help you please the family without spending the entire evening in the kitchen. In addition there are hundreds of tips and ideas to help you keep your sanity, including:

- Ten cooking basics every mom must know
- Fun ways kids can help in the kitchen
- Plan-ahead meals that can be prepared on the weekend
- Tips on prepping, cooking, and freezing
- And much more!

ISBN 0-7615-1458-9 / paperback / 240 pages
U.S. $15.00 / Can. $22.00

To order, call (800) 632-8676 or visit us online at www.primapublishing.com

INTERNATIONAL CONVERSION CHART

These are not exact equivalents: they've been slightly rounded to make measuring easier.

LIQUID MEASUREMENTS

American	Imperial	Metric	Australian
2 tablespoons (1 oz.)	1 fl. oz.	30 ml	1 tablespoon
¼ cup (2 oz.)	2 fl. oz.	60 ml	2 tablespoons
⅓ cup (3 oz.)	3 fl. oz.	80 ml	¼ cup
½ cup (4 oz.)	4 fl. oz.	125 ml	⅓ cup
⅔ cup (5 oz.)	5 fl. oz.	165 ml	½ cup
¾ cup (6 oz.)	6 fl. oz.	185 ml	⅔ cup
1 cup (8 oz.)	8 fl. oz.	250 ml	¾ cup

SPOON MEASUREMENTS

American	Metric
¼ teaspoon	1 ml
½ teaspoon	2 ml
1 teaspoon	5 ml
1 tablepoon	15 ml

OVEN TEMPERATURES

Fahrenheit	Centigrade	Gas
250	120	½
300	150	2
325	160	3
350	180	4
375	190	5
400	200	6
450	230	8

WEIGHTS

US/UK	Metric
1 oz.	30 grams (g)
2 oz.	60 g
4 oz. (¼ lb)	125 g
5 oz. (⅓ lb)	155 g
6 oz.	185 g
7 oz.	220 g
8 oz. (½ lb)	250 g
10 oz.	315 g
12 oz. (¾ lb)	375 g
14 oz.	440 g
16 oz. (1 lb)	500 g
2 lbs.	1 kg